With a
Black Platoon
in Combat

TEXAS A&M UNIVERSITY

29

MILITARY HISTORY SERIES

With a Black Platoon in Combat

A YEAR IN KOREA

Lyle Rishell

Texas A&M University Press
College Station

The paper used in this book meets the minimum requirements of the American National Standard for Permanence of Paper for Printed Library Materials, Z39.48-1984. Binding materials have been chosen for durability.
∞

Library of Congress Cataloging-in-Publication Data

Rishell, Lyle, 1927–
    With a Black Platoon in combat : a year in Korea / Lyle Rishell.
        p.   cm. – (Texas A&M University military history series : no. 29)
    Includes index.
    ISBN 0-89096-526-9
    1. Rishell, Lyle, 1927– . 2. Korean War, 1950–1953 – Personal narratives, American.   3. Afro-American soldiers – Korea. I. Title.
II. Series: Texas A&M University military history series ; 29.
DS921.6.R57   1983
951.904′2′092 – dc20   92-27918
                                            CIP

This story is dedicated to the memory of the men
who fought in the 24th Infantry Regiment
and all the support groups that
helped make our lives a bit easier.

He who thinks of war as being a necessary evil is insane;
he who fights in war knows that war itself is indeed insane.

Contents

Illustrations

Preface

Histories of war, and the men and women who served in them, are often seen as an accumulation of memories that offer a catharsis for the writer. Sometimes historians attempt to paint a grand picture of the events of the day in order to purge a nation's conscience. This story does neither. It has been some forty years since the outbreak of the Korean War, and I am not attempting to write a historical account of what was called Truman's Police Action, nor am I rewriting the history of the 24th Infantry Regiment.

This is a story about Korea, and of a black platoon of Able Company, 24th Infantry Regiment. It was the single black regiment to fight in Korea that had not been integrated, although several black battalions arrived later and went into action. The troops were commanded for the most part by white officers, which in itself was unique.

It is also a tale of honor and heroism and spirit, of death and dying, and of the cries of wounded men. That they were black is important. They fought and died for their country and gave of themselves to the last full measure. They performed well. There was never a moment when they failed me, nor did I give any thought to the fact that they were black. As their white platoon leader, company executive officer, and battalion staff officer, I lived with them, led many into battle, suffered with them, and came home with those who survived.

The story evolved from notes I made during the period of June 1950 to late May 1951. Parts of the story are not too pretty, and I have omitted certain parts of the narrative that might offend the sensibilities of the reader. Clearest in my memory are the battles and moments of danger; the times between were etched less surely. I have tried to be objective and accurate in my reporting, but if there are errors in the story, they are neither intentional nor meant to mislead. Above all, this is a true chronicle that needs to be told the way I saw it happen.

I have attempted to describe the situations and circumstances of an infantry platoon in action. The events and people I tell about here are just like those of many small units of the army and the marines as they fought a ground battle in the mountains and valleys of Korea. In all cases my notes were made during or immediately after the particular operation, and I have tried not to analyze them or to improve upon the action described. War is not pretty, and to attempt to beautify it would defeat the purpose.

While some will not agree with what I have written, and may even accuse me of embellishing the facts, the details of war as I experienced them are real: the black soldier can be very proud of his devotion to duty and the battles he fought in my unit in Korea.

Korean War Chronology

June 25, 1950	Communist troops of the People's Democratic Republic of Korea invade South Korea.
June 26	United Nations Security Council demands that North Korea withdraw troops north of the 38th Parallel.
June 27	President Truman orders U.S. air and naval forces to assist in defending South Korea.
June 28	North Korean forces attack and take Seoul.
June 30	The president orders U.S. ground forces into action.
August 3	UN troops, after a general withdrawal, set up the Pusan Perimeter in the southeastern tip of Korea.
September 15	UN offensive commences with the invasion of Inchon.
September 19	UN forces jump off from the Pusan Perimeter.
September 25	UN forces recapture Seoul.
October 19	UN forces capture Pyongyang, capital of North Korea.
October 25	Chinese Communists enter the war.
November 26	Chinese and North Korean armies halt UN offensive, and a general withdrawal commences.
January 4, 1951	Communists recapture and occupy Seoul.
March 15	UN forces recapture Seoul.
April 11	MacArthur is removed from command and is replaced by Gen. Matthew Ridgway as supreme commander.
July 10	Peace talks begin, but fighting continues.
January 3, 1952	Communists reject a proposal for voluntary repatriation of prisoners of war.

April 28   Gen. Mark Clark replaces Ridgway, who
                    replaces General Eisenhower in
                    Europe.
October 8   Truce talks are broken off at Panmunjom.
March 28, 1953   Communists accept a proposal for ex-
                    change of wounded and sick POWs.
April 21   Exchange of prisoners commences.
April 26   Peace talks resume.
July 27   Truce agreement is signed; all fighting
                    ends.

With a
Black Platoon
in Combat

1. Alpha Phase

On June 25, 1950, with the blessing of the Soviets, the North Korean high command ordered its military forces to launch a full-scale invasion across the 38th Parallel against the Republic of Korea. That demarcation line, established after World War II, had been created for the sole purpose of accepting the Japanese surrender. Because the Soviet Union had declared war on Japan two days after the United States dropped the bomb on Hiroshima, the USSR established itself as the occupying power in North Korea. It was not, as has been suggested, a liberating army; it had not fought its way into Korea.

Korea had experienced foreign troops many times. In its ancient history it had been invaded by Chinese, Mongols, Manchus, and Japanese. For centuries the Chinese had exerted much influence over Korea. Then three and one-half centuries before UN forces arrived, the Japanese invaded through the port city of Pusan. After the combined Korean-Chinese armies had ejected the Japanese, Korea refused the overtures of other foreign states and sealed itself off from the rest of the world. In doing so, it insulated its people and developed and retained an independent way of life unique to Korea. It became the "Hermit Kingdom," and while it remained poor in worldly goods, it had its own language, culture, literature, and national ambitions. Not until the nineteenth century did it reopen its ports and permit international trade.

The opening of its doors was a signal to China, Japan, and Russia that Korea was up for grabs. China considered Korea to be a buffer between itself and Japan. The Japanese had eyed the peninsula for years because it provided a strategic approach to the mainland (Manchuria and China). Russia, not to be outdone, wanted Korea as a convenient land bridge into Southeast Asia.

The countries opted for war. By the end of the century the Japanese had beaten the Chinese and had become a greater influence over Korea than China. But still Japan's objective of giving Korea its independence, under Japanese influence, was unfulfilled, and Japan attacked again. Finally, after defeating the Russians in

1905, Japan made Korea a protectorate, and then, with a flourish, formally annexed the country in 1910. From that time until 1945 Japan ruled Korea as a fiefdom and governed the peninsula to further its own interests in every sense of the word.

With the end of World War II the Soviets had finally won, without a fight, the opportunity to gain a foothold easily and quickly on the long sought-after peninsula. Once there, they effectively and without further delay set up a puppet government, the People's Democratic Republic of Korea, and named Kim Il Sung as prime minister. Thus, North Korea was occupied quickly, and the anticipated freedom that should have come to the Korean people with the surrender of the Japanese never materialized.

Between 1945 and the outbreak of the war, both parts of Korea could not reconcile their political differences to become one nation. Nor was there any intent to establish two zones of occupation. The Soviets maintained North Korea as a satellite state, created a Communist constitution, stifled political dissent, and established a military, political, and economic enclave subservient to Moscow. There had never been any agreement that Korea should be divided into two states, but in the vacuum created by the subsequent withdrawal of U.S. forces from the south, and with the forcefulness of the Soviet regime's rejection of U.S. proposals made to the Joint Soviet-U.S. Commission, the 38th Parallel became the de facto division of the country. The fact is that both parts of Korea were considered to be unofficial protectorates of the occupying powers.

There is little doubt that the Soviets had conceived and swiftly executed a plan that encompassed their goals of expansion in the Far East. Their timetable, which included declaration of war on Japan, their forceful entry into North Korea in order to set up a Communist government, and their repeated intransigence in resolving the issue of a united Korea, proceeded on schedule, and it appeared there was little the Western powers could do to delay or stop the ultimate division.

After all, the West had remained at a safe distance as the Russians moved into Eastern Europe to establish satellite Communist states. The United States was not prepared to get into a fight with the Soviets so soon after World War II, and the Soviets were masters of the art of subverting or controlling people in states that had just gone through, or were in the midst of, socioeconomic or political crisis.

The inability of the two powers to reach an agreement on the independence of all Korea did not bode well for the future of the country. For two years, maneuvering for a political resolution continued in the joint commission. Finally, despairing of success in the face of the Soviet position, the United States in 1947 set the issue before the United Nations, which quickly called for national elections open to both North and South Korea for the following year.

The Soviets refused to honor the free elections in the North. In the South, however, a national assembly was elected, a democratic constitution was drawn, a president was elected, and the Republic of Korea was formally and legally established. The Soviets refused to accept the Republic of Korea as the legally constituted and valid government in Korea. Not surprisingly, when the issue was presented to the United Nations, the Soviets vetoed membership of the republic.

The Soviet plan to subvert and control all of Korea was on schedule, although they had their work cut out for them. With uncanny foresight, they proceeded to strengthen their position in North Korea. While they had ostensibly withdrawn the bulk of their armed forces from Korea in late 1948, there remained a cadre of advisers of every sort – political, economic, and military – who were instructed to make the country into a puppet state.

At about the same time, the withdrawal of U.S. occupation troops commenced, and by June 1949 only a small group of American advisers remained behind to train Korean security forces. The Soviets concluded, and perhaps rightfully so, that the United States no longer wished to maintain a military presence in Korea, a situation that placed the country up for grabs again.

The USSR, failing in its attempt to make all of Korea into a Communist state, commenced with a vengeance to separate the two parts and to remold North Korea into its own sphere. Almost immediately, but not without great effort, the North Korean regime closed off the 38th Parallel and stopped traffic into and out of North Korea. The demarcation line now became the political boundary between North and South. At the same time, a North Korean army was established, training initiated, and equipment provided. The military buildup commenced in earnest. The Soviets provided individual weapons, artillery pieces, and even aircraft, while in the South the United States withheld heavy weapons and other offensive equipment from the Korean army. Commercial activities between the two states stopped. The Communists severed the political-economic relationship without pause. The social structure was revamped in accordance with Communist ideology: the welfare of the state was more important than that of the individual, and the rights of the individual were governed and superseded by the state. In its long history of foreign domination, North Korea would come to accept still another country imposing its will over the people. And there was little the United States or the family of the United Nations could do about it.

Now began the last stage in the master plan before the invasion: the disruption of the political, economic, and social structures of the newly proclaimed Republic of Korea. Without constraints placed upon them, the North Koreans, urged on by their masters in Russia and on-the-ground advisers, initiated a series of actions to undermine the confidence of the South Korean people in their new government. Terrorist groups crossed into South Korea almost at will. Invariably, they attempted to influence the South Koreans in such a way that doubts were spread about the officials of the government and their ability to govern. These concerns were exacerbated by propaganda machines in the north, which pumped out a litany of outright lies, half-truths, and vitriolic attacks upon the government.

Realizing that these actions were insufficient in and of themselves to cause a collapse of government, the North Korean army launched a series of attacks across the 38th Parallel, again aimed at bringing unification to the peninsula. Some of these were large-scale military operations, but although the South Koreans were poorly equipped, they were successful in repulsing the raids. In view of the fact that no additional rearming of South Korea was undertaken, one can only speculate that these actions were shrugged off by the United States as being insignificant and that the United States and the United Nations retained the belief that some peaceful solution would be proposed and would be acceptable to all sides. That the outside world did not take notice of what was happening in North Korea until after the invasion demonstrates the utter confusion and frustration that was endemic in the formulation of the United States' political strategy.

While overall U.S. strategy was merely to provide economic aid and technical assistance to South Korea to assist that country to get back on its feet after the long occupation by the Japanese, the Soviets were creating an armed camp with the goal of overrunning South Korea and moving on into the rest of Asia. Technical aid was provided, but the Soviets focused on every possible way to disrupt the lower republic, using propaganda, strikes, border raids, sabotage, restrictions on economic or social contacts, and other methods. And while the Republic of Korea was the obvious target, the Soviets had a free hand in North Korea and continued to run that territory as a serfdom of Communism.

Finally, the time was ripe. The North Korean peace petitions, which formed the basis for the unification proposal, were now floated. They called for new national elections to be held in both North and South Korea in early August 1950. Whether that call was a smokescreen to keep South Korea off-guard or whether the Communists really believed the UN commission would go along with the proposal and were prepared to make concessions is disputable. In view of every action they had taken previously, I believe they were ready for war and knew that the only way out was to attack. They did not make a preemptive strike in order to precipitate an attack from South Korea. Rather, it was a carefully planned and calculated move to unify all of Korea by force.

Although the political-military focus at that time was on Western Europe, on June 29 President Truman authorized deployment of ground, air, and naval forces to assist in defending South Korea. This was the first time that a president, as commander-in-chief of the armed forces, made a commitment to use Americans without a declaration of war.

In view of the happenings in Eastern Europe, and particularly the use of raw power being displayed by the Soviets, it is surprising that the United States drew the line. If it failed to confront the aggression in Korea, the USSR would continue its provocative acts. At the same time, the fear of another world war permeated the political life of our leaders, and Truman did not want to see Korea escalate into a large-scale battle. Thus he characterized the commitment as a "police action," a phrase that became almost a term of derision to the troops being sent into action.

Before his order, however, the United States had called for an emergency meeting of the United Nations, at which time the United States requested that that body declare the move by North Korea to be illegal and provide for the defense of South Korea. On July 7 the Security Council agreed that the flag of the United Nations would be the banner under which the various member states could provide support. This decision resulted in the creation of the United Nations Command, headed by Gen. Douglas MacArthur.

The transition from an occupying power in Japan to war strength and fighting capability was not easily made or readily implemented. There were perhaps a few hundred men in the advisory force in Korea, but as noted earlier, their primary mission was to assist in the training of security forces. These forces themselves did not have much in the way of equipment, and their training was by the very nature of things, oriented toward defense. U.S. military policy at that time was limited to providing only light weapons to South Korea, so there was no way that South Korea could carry a war to the North. There were several justifications for that military posture: (1) the United States believed there was a greater possibility of war breaking out in other parts of the world, particularly on Formosa (Taiwan); (2) the government did not want to give South Korea the capability to attack North Korea; (3) following World War II there was continuing pressure to reduce U.S. forces around the world with a concomitant reduction in defense expenditures; and (4) the United States was by then the world's largest producer of goods and services, and supplies were being shipped throughout the world to assist in rebuilding devastated economies left by the war.

The North Korean attack found the U.S. forces wanting. As a nation, we were dismally unprepared for another war so soon or so far away. When the president responded, requesting that member nations in the United Nations oppose the North Koreans in order to restore peace in Korea, he had few fighting divisions; those which were closest to the action were all understrength, partially equipped, and, for the most part, made up of men who had not seen action in World War II. We were, in short, hardly prepared to conduct war in the summer of 1950.

There were few trained and fully equipped ground forces available for rapid deployment. In Japan and elsewhere, under the austerity program instituted by Secretary of Defense Louis Johnson, all active army and marine combat divisions were understrength, except for one in Europe. Divisions consisted of two regiments of the three authorized, and in Japan the regiments contained only two battalions. As a result of this reduction, officers and men were immediately assigned or reassigned to flesh out and supplement the 24th and 25th infantry divisions. This appeared to be a rational and prudent move, since at the time, the United States had no way of knowing whether this would be a prolonged attack on South Korea, or whether Communist strategy focused on a broader sphere of action.

Nevertheless, the immediate action undertaken by the United States was to dispatch a task force of the 24th Infantry Division by air to Korea on July 2, and it engaged North Korean forces on July 5. It was the first move by opposing forces, one that would be repeated many times during the first year of the war. At the time I was ordered south, I had no knowledge of this, or of the fact that the 25th Infantry had been alerted and was organizing for follow-on departure.

I wonder if perhaps the Soviets' long-range planning might have been flawed, and without Moscow's blessing a misguided Kim Il Sung decided not to wait for the elections and struck out on his own account. If so, could the Soviet masters call off their dogs or admit to the world that they could not control them?

In any event, it was the first move in a game of checkers, of moves and countermoves that would continue for thirty-seven months. In the end, both players had to settle for a truce.

2. Mobilization and Movement

On the same day that South Korea was invaded, I arrived in Yokohama, Japan, from an assignment in a small camp located on the
northern coast of the island of Honshu, across the strait from Hok-
kaido. In Yokohama I was to await passage on a ship to the United
States. My days with the army in the Far East Command were fast
coming to an end, and I had received my scheduled portcall for
July 9. I eagerly anticipated the free time I would have in Tokyo
before leaving Japan.

The following day we received the news. At first, those of us
ready to board a ship in a few days could not understand the significance of the conflict in Korea, nor were we ready mentally even
to think about the possibility of being reassigned. It never entered
our heads. Korea was still far away; it was of little concern to us,
and we disposed of it as something, I suppose, that would have
to be worked out between the two parties. We were completely
unaware of the political problems that had finally reached the point
of no return between North and South Korea, and the battle that
was now in progress was of little interest.

The decision made by President Truman to commit ground,
air, and naval forces changed our world; as soon as we received
word that the president had ordered U.S. military forces to come
to the aid of South Korea, our views changed. Now we expected
that our orders would be amended, and in fact, within a few days
the sailing orders were canceled, and reassignment orders issued.
I was ordered to report to a replacement depot outside of Tokyo
on the main island of Honshu.

When I arrived and had reported in, there was mass confusion. Troops were milling around the compound, wondering when
they were leaving. Some had orders to report to units, while others
waited. The depot staff, which generally operated as an incoming
headquarters for replacements arriving from the United States, now
found itself charged with diverting troops to the most southern
military units, which had already received alert orders.

The first unit to be alerted was the U.S. 24th Infantry Division, closely followed by the 25th Infantry Division, both of which occupied geographic positions in Japan closer to Korea. Within a day or so I was on my way again, this time to the 25th Division. The division was being deployed to Korea and was in the process of being brought up to reasonable strength in men, equipment, and various war materiel.

I wondered at the time what was happening at Camp Haugen, and whether the 7th Infantry Division, which I had just departed had been alerted too. When I had joined it months before, Col. Beauchamp was the commanding officer (CO) of the 32d Regiment and Lt. Col. Charles Mount was commanding the 1st Battalion. Of Beauchamp I remember little, but Mount was a tall, lean officer who was soft-spoken and articulate. As a young lieutenant, I did not have many occasions to talk with him, but he appeared to be a friendly person whom the men respected as a commander. The regiment had stressed frequent training exercises, both in garrison and the field, and I spent many days and nights in the field while there. Now I fully expected the training to pay off, and I was convinced that we were moving into a royal battle. Knowing that I was being shipped out as a replacement officer, and not with my old unit, did little to soothe my apprehension at that moment. The thought surfaced that if my portcall had been delayed by two weeks, I would still be with the 7th Division. But those were the breaks one gets, and I pushed the unpleasantness aside. It was time to move on.

It was a hot and humid July afternoon when I arrived at my destination. It was a railroad marshaling yard somewhere south of Tokyo. It would be an understatement to note that it was chaotic, a scene remembered only because of the number of people trying to make sense out of disarray and confusion. The sun beat down on the tracks and the loading docks, and men and officers were running and shouting; vehicles were moving everywhere unloading, and the Japanese were scurrying to and fro. Engines were trying to push and pull freight cars into some kind of train arrangement to be ready for departure and the commingling of equipment, people, and voices and the smell of burning coal and spouting steam were overwhelming. There was an urgency and precious little rest for the men as they darted around in sweat-soaked shirts and dripping bodies to finish loading the train before dark. Special Service workers were handing out cold drinks and offering coffee and doughnuts to the troops. But there was still time for a lot of joking and laughing; the war was light-miles away.

In retrospect, I believe that I could have disappeared in that melee and never would have been missed. I suspect that when I was issued orders, they were open ended and were worded to the effect that I was to proceed to some Rail Transportation Office (RTO) for further movement to a port of debarkation. To whom I was to report and when were probably spelled out, but I have no memory of the details. Like a good soldier, I did not question the orders and never thought of making a disappearing act. I wonder now what the outcome might have been if I had failed to report in until some later date, and which unit I would have joined before leaving for Korea. But the dice had been rolled, and I came up with a winner.

The afternoon wore on. Time was drawing short. As dusk descended, the supplies had been loaded and the vehicles blocked and tied down on the flatcars. The orders were then passed to check our personal equipment – weapons, ammunition loads, bedrolls, and rations. All excess gear that had not already been stowed with our units or, in my case, shipped home, was packed in cartons and held at the holding point. It was the last I would see of my possessions.

There is something permanent about giving up clothing and other articles that one would have little need of in Korea, a feeling of offering a part of your life. I had the least to give up, since I had packed earlier for leaving the country, and I was certain that when I arrived in San Francisco, I would be needing my civilian clothes and other things I had accumulated in Japan. One might think that I agonized over the distribution of my effects, that I was ambivalent about what I wanted to take with me and what I wanted to leave behind. There was no such agony. I packed the carton and my suitcase, tagged them, and turned them over. I retained what I felt I could use, and that was it. As an infantryman, I knew I would have to haul and hustle my own belongings, and I think I was smart enough to know that we might face some forced marches as soon as we got to Korea, so I packed lightly.

When it was dark, the men were assigned to coaches, while the drivers of the assigned vehicles were to ride on the flatcars with their vehicles. A few soldiers rode in the baggage car, and the small group of officers opted to ride in one of the empty boxcars.

There were seven of us in the group, and we spread out our gear and made pallets on the floor. The senior officer was a lieutenant colonel from the Adjutant General Corps, and among the rest there was a Jewish chaplain, a personnel officer from some outfit who barely made the train, and four lieutenants. One was a Signal Corps type, and the rest were infantry. My military occupation specialty (MOS) was small-unit commander, so I was far from being reassured to find myself heading south on my way to Korea. I did not have to be a genius to guess that I was going into combat; one moves in that direction only because of a war.

There was no dearth of rumors and stories about what was happening in Korea. I found myself drawn to the chaplain, with whom I could not relate either professionally or spiritually, but for some reason I distanced myself from the others, with whom I had much more in common. For the most part, they were in the same situation as I was. Some sat in the car oblivious to what was happening around them; they had said good-bye to loved ones and did not want conversation to intrude upon their thoughts. Others of the group wanted or needed to share their thoughts, and they never stopped talking. So many questions were asked in an attempt to make sense out of the future. And as many answers were given, not because anyone knew or was knowledgeable about where we were going, but because the speakers wished to confirm their own hopes and fears.

Some thought we'd wait for our units in Sasebo before being sent to Korea. Others objected to the idea of going in the first place, thinking that the Koreans ought to be fighting their own war. Others thought the war wasn't going to last very long. They had heard that we would be home for Christmas, that we're just going there as part of the UN, to help out, and then we'd come home.

There was something disturbing about the confused questions being asked and the unconvincing answers being offered. While I was angry at being reassigned at the moment I was scheduled to rotate to the United States, I had come to accept the way the dice had rolled for me and found no comfort in what was being said. I knew without really knowing that we were going into combat; my every sense screamed back at me that this was not going to be "just a police action." I knew that what I would be thrust into was precisely what I had been trained for since Fort Benning. My mortality was not a consideration at this point; that would change as I experienced battle. I pushed aside the thoughts being expressed and found peace with myself and, by extension, the U.S. Army, which had changed my orders, placed me on this train, and started me on a voyage from which I would emerge a changed person.

A flurry of activity caught my attention. The troops were milling around waiting to be called into formation for the roll call. A train commander along with a couple of sergeants were moving from one car to another to check the lashings and the blocks on the flatcars. Several loads had to be tied down again, but for the most part the work was finished. The American soldier, probably like his counterpart around the world, always seems to be ready to get into trouble whenever he has a few minutes to while away the time. Now they were bartering some personal items. Some were hassling the crowd of Japanese, like a barker at the circus, trying to drum up attention for the auction underway. Unfortunately, the noise they made reached the train commander, and since he was responsible for the troop count, he interrupted the game and had them called to attention. Then the roll was called, and each non-com escorted a group to the assigned coach and loaded them.

The train started moving at last. Amid the noise and confusion and the knowledge that we were leaving the known for whatever lay ahead, there was an overwhelming need to reach out one last time to the Japanese people who had come to see us off. There was this feeling of finality, the last tenuous thread of continuity in our lives, before entering into the future unknown. I believe we all wanted to say good-bye to someone, and the Japanese who had befriended us showed their love and concern for us as we moved slowly along the platform.

I watched the platform slide past, and then, as the train picked up speed, we were left with a loneliness that permeated our thoughts. How long would we be gone? What challenges lay ahead? Would we ever see this land again? Was this trip the beginning of the end for some of us, or all of us? We knew our destination instead of our destinies. Who could imagine that night on the train what really lay before us? I suspect there were many who thought the same thoughts, deep within his soul.

It was a long train of cars, made up of boxcars, flatcars, loaded with an assortment of vehicles, and passenger cars. The coaches were poorly equipped; they held narrow, straight-backed seats, and the men were hot and dirty and uncomfortable, but they complained little. Many spent the evening reading or gambling, and a few looked out at the villages flashing past, alone with their thoughts. Long after it had gotten dark, and after our eyes started to smart from the smoke of the engine pouring into the open door, we spread our blankets on the floor and tried to sleep. The men used whatever little space they could find between the aisles as their berths. The train rattled and rolled throughout the night, but the clacking of the wheels precluded anything more than a brief catnap as we roared on through Kyushu and further south.

At daybreak we pulled into some nondescript station and were allowed off the train to stretch our limbs. A few Japanese vendors were out early, and we were able to buy some candy and chewing gum before loading again and moving out. We broke open our C rations, brewed coffee on a hibachi that someone had thoughtfully packed aboard, and watched the sun move higher in the sky as we continued. Our spirits rose with the food, and there was a lot of bantering and laughter.

As we passed yet another station, someone had scrawled across a sign, "Kilroy was here," and someone in the car yelled, "You guys never had it so good!" And another, "Nor so often!" This elicited a round of laughter, which was good for the soul.

Most of us had little knowledge about Korea. We did know that the Japanese had occupied it for years and that Korea had regained its independence only after the war. We tried to visualize what we would find, and it was the consensus that Korea was pretty backward, a place studded with rice paddies and mountains. As for the weather there, we hadn't the foggiest idea, although some senior sage in the car suggested it was going to be just like Japan. I expected it to be a terrifying place and expressed myself, but for the most part, the members of our group were not quite ready to accept the notion. I could not be dissuaded from my perception. Indeed, before long I found that I was not far wrong.

We had kept the door of the boxcar open all night, and as the day wore on and the car became quite warm, we formed a circle around the opening. By leaning out a bit, we could watch the train move around the curves in the road. The engine kept belching great clouds of black smoke. The cinders in it would make our eyes sting, and we would withdraw to let someone else look. The GIs were hanging out of every opening, watching the villages and the farms flash by.

Almost everywhere we looked, the Japanese stopped whatever they were doing and waved and shouted to us. Maybe they were expressing their happiness at seeing us leave, but I do not think so. From the station where we loaded to the port of Sasebo, there were masses of people at nearly all of the stations wishing us good-bye. As we slipped past the industrialized cities, the small, sleepy villages, and the fishing towns, they were there. Past the stunted hills rising from the flatlands below, through endless miles of terraced rice paddies and small farms, the working people offered us their wishes. Only a few short years earlier, they might have watched their own sons and fathers go off to war.

A unique and rather emotional scene was yet to come. As we rolled through Kyushu and slowed to pass through a station on the main line, a very old and wrinkled woman saw us standing in the door of the boxcar. Already on her knees, she clasped her worn hands together, bowed her head, and moved her lips in prayer. She tore our hearts with that simple gesture. For me, it was an example of love and a commitment to the Americans, for herself, and for the future. Few of us doubted the sincerity of these people. Her expression of concern affected all of us. The Japanese had not forgotten. From the sidewalks and schools, from houses standing within an arm's length from the tracks, from the factory gates and the farms, a gentle, gracious people gave us all they had to offer – a hand of friendship and their blessings.

On July 8, we arrrived in Sasebo. It was a fairly large city on the tip of Kyushu, where the U.S. Navy occupied a large naval base. The train did not stop until we got to the port. It was midafternoon under a scalding sun as the unloading commenced. As the vehicles were untied from the flatcars, they were driven to the ship and loaded aboard the vessel. The men struggled with the loading most of the day.

By no stretch of the imagination could the *Kango Maru* be considered a luxury liner. At the time, I believe that it was probably one of the few ships available to the Americans. The *Kango Maru* was a ferryboat, capacity unknown, a squatty-looking ship, run down at the heels. It was streaked with rust along the hull and low in the water, and my initial impression was one of apprehension; I was not convinced that it was the vessel that was to carry me to Korea. The wheelhouse was painted a dull tan, but the overall appearance was also dull. The first view of it that afternoon in July was anything but an illusion. It did ferry me, along with many others, across the Korea Strait to the "Land of the Morning Calm."

All afternoon there were hectic preparations to load and stash aboard the equipment and supplies for combat. Much of the gear was placed in the holds to provide stability to the ship, while the vehicles were secured on deck in various places. Since a ferry is made for people, storage space seemed to be at a premium; there was little wasted room. By the time we got the ammunition and rations aboard, it was well into the late afternoon, and the sun was getting low.

The Red Cross workers were all over the place. They had prepared soup and sandwiches, hot coffee and doughnuts. "Dough-nut Dollies" could be found everywhere, always willing to help, offering their services with a friendly smile. I am sure that as the war progressed and more troops were embarked through Sasebo, they were able to refine the system, but at that time it appeared to be jerry-built and chaotic at best. Nevertheless, it was good to see the Grey Ladies (the Red Cross Auxiliary) and have a few minutes to talk to them before leaving. They possessed boundless energy, and just by being there they made our leaving a little bit easier.

The officers making the trip were assigned to ride herd on the men and were told the specific areas in the ship where they would be housed for the crossing. Then we received instructions about eating, smoking, and schedules for going on deck. As soon as we started to load, the horseplay and joking stopped. The men got pretty serious. I moved up the gangplank and onto the ship. We were struck with a terrible smell. The scent of people being ferried from place to place for years must have permeated the woodwork and the mats, and that odor, combined with diesel oil to fire the boilers, was nearly overpowering. The smell from the heads added to the stench and made me feel about ready to throw up.

It was far worse on the lower level where the men were placed in large, windowless bays that looked like livestock holding pens, except that they were covered with tatami mats, a rice-straw floor covering. After further search, my group found a smaller section of the boat, which at least was farther from the heads, and throwing our gear onto the mats, we escaped back to the deck for some fresh air.

After some delay, the lines were cast off and pulled onto the deck. There was some cheering from the people on shore, but for the most part, the troops were pretty quiet. It was not a happy departure. Many of the men had left sweethearts behind, while a few had said good-bye to wives and children, and the hurt was deep as they said their farewells. Perhaps many, as I did, wondered if they would ever see Japan again. The *Kango Maru* was finally underway.

As the lights of Sasebo faded in the distance, the men grew even more silent. There must be some kind of catharsis in withdrawing into one's own shell, not needing to talk to anyone. There is comfort in being alone and in not having anyone or anything intrude upon one's thoughts. When we were far from shore, the blackness descended around us and the stars shone bright. There was nothing else; the loneliness was palpable.

A few of us remained on deck for hours, reluctant to leave the peacefulness of this final night to go below. Then the deck slowly emptied of the men, and we went in search of our bay, unrolled our blankets, and tried to sleep on the rolling, pitching ship.

3. Korea, the Hermit Kingdom

All night long the ship chugged along toward Korea, and at dawn, as the sun was rising in the East, we slowly came into the port of Pusan. The ferryboat sputtered and slowed, then jockeyed alongside a pier, and finally came to a stop. I cannot forget my first impression. The overall view from the deck was most displeasing and not very encouraging. As far as one could see, which was the port area alone, the colors were black and gray and olive drab. There was no brightness to light the scene; the buildings, the people, the clutter, and the military supplies being off-loaded and stacked on the ground were all the same dull shade, with few exceptions.

Looking down, I could see Korean dock workers laboriously filling small, shallow baskets with coal to fire the boilers on the return trip. Some were even wearing white, a color we soon found to be prevalent throughout Korea, although I wondered why it should be worn in a coal heap. Glancing aft from where I stood, I took pictures of the men working to untie the deck loads so that the off-loading could commence. Pusan was the largest port in Korea, and many other vessels lay nearby, refueling or waiting to deposit their loads onto the overburdened quay. But wonder of wonders, there was not the rich, unwelcome smell to overpower the senses that I had experienced on my arrival in Japan. Later I learned that night soil was not used generally in the built-up areas; rather, fertilizer and compost were more common. Nevertheless, the same cloying, disgusting smell returned as soon as we reached the countryside.

We quietly disembarked from the *Kango Maru* and marched to some assembly area near the port. There appeared to be a lot of confusion, but I suspect it was a question more of getting organized than of disarray. The initial contingent of troops had just arrived and was being processed for the front. In what had been a primary school (or so the sign stated), the soldiers had placed crossed flags of the United States and Korea above the first-floor entrance. A sign below proclaimed, "Welcome U.S. Army," a simple reminder of where we had finally arrived. It was our first look at the national

Rear-echelon support troops, July 9, 1950. *Author's photograph*

flag: a red and blue circle, called a yin-yang, on a white field (for peace and purity), with slanted black bars placed at each corner of the background.

So this is Korea, I thought. And these are the people. They did not look like the Japanese or the Chinese. They had a broader face and straight black hair and dark eyes. They appeared to be an admixture, and as I was to learn later, they are different ethnically from both the Chinese and the Japanese. This was a port area, and the people swarming around looked to be quite poor. Poverty was written on their faces and what they wore, and their lethargy seemed to permeate their very souls. I did not see among them the hustle and bustle of the Japanese. Perhaps they were still in shock, trying to comprehend the invasion from the north, or again, they may have been completely uninformed about the United Nations resolution that would maintain the integrity of their republic. Then again, perhaps they resented still another invasion, for whatever reasons and regardless of what had happened in the North, and they saw us as an uninvited power that could destroy their culture and rape and plunder the land once more.

What was this place where we now found ourselves? What cultural differences would we find? What constituted its social, economic, and political life? What kind of terrain and weather would face us? How would the people react to us? Would they perceive us as another invading force, or welcome us? These and dozens of other questions floated through my mind, but the answers came slowly, and frequently not at all.

We learned quickly that Korea was a peninsula that juts into the Sea of Japan and that it was divided politically into the People's Democratic Republic in the North, and the Republic of Korea in the South. Its population was about thirty million people, 75 percent of whom were farmers. It appeared to be a tragically poor country, with little industrial development in the southern portion. The major population density was centered on the western side of the peninsula, where the land configuration provided the arable land for agriculture. The eastern half was a land of mountains and valleys, a formidable obstacle to the fighting we were soon to face.

In the short time we spent in Japan before shipping out, we had not learned much about Korea. We did know that under Japanese rule some of the land had been sold to Japanese settlers, and the native Koreans had to scratch their existence out of small parcels of land that were left. One of the first observations, confirmed over and over as we traveled Korea, was that Koreans had little love for the Japanese. During the preceding forty years the Japanese had taken over the industrial base, had stripped the forests (at least in South Korea), had mined the minerals, and had even exported the people back to Japan. There is no question but that

Korea became a source of food, wood, and minerals for the expansionary objectives of the Japanese in the Pacific region.

It became increasingly clear that Korea had been stripped. With the exception of the highlands, there was nothing but scrub brush, and most of the hills showed serious erosion. As we started north, the systematic rape of the country became visible. There are no pictures in my possession today that show anything less.

The producers of rice, the farmers, did not appear to utilize the land quite as efficiently as did the Japanese. While there were terraced fields, they did not appear to be as abundant as those we saw in Japan. Korean agriculture is labor-intensive; in all the areas and in every region I passed through, I never saw anything but the crudest kinds of farming implements. There were no large expanses of farmland that I remember, and yet Korea, under the Japanese, had been a net exporting country of rice. I could not imagine that crop yields were high, for many of the farmers whom I saw were gathering and threshing grain and winnowing it by hand as I suspect they had been doing for centuries. Rice and barley appeared to be the principal food crops, although we frequently found fields of sorghum. Only once did we pass through an orchard, but the apples we found were small and worm-ridden and did not offer us much sustenance. Of the vegetables, the most common were cabbage, onions, and a white tuberous turnip or radish, all of which formed the Korean hot-pickle dish known as kimchi. This national staple was not to my liking or, for that matter, to any of the Americans'.

Outside the major cities of Pusan, Seoul, Taejon, Taegu, Kunsan, and Suwon that I traveled through (and that were fairly scattered), the style and construction of the buildings was primitive. In the larger cities, brick and wood were used; in the countryside, nearly every house was built using cornstalks plastered with mud to form the walls, and their floors were heated by passages underneath that allowed the smoke to circulate before going up the flue. It was actually a very efficient system, and on several occasions I found the houses to be quite comfortable. Still, the peasantry lived at a subsistence level. While I never saw anyone with the signs of starvation, the daily diet of rice and kimchi could not have been totally adequate. A few times we saw chickens, but I never saw a pig or goat, and only twice did I catch a glimpse of a cow. For all of that, my overall impression was that the villagers and farmers had adjusted well to an ill-tempered climate in a most inhospitable environment that provided their existence.

Korea was divided, not only from north to south, but from west to east. The western half of the peninsula constituted the plains region, where the population density was the highest, and where the bulk of the agriculture was undertaken. Here we found terraces holding rice crops, and dry farmlands, but from every point on the compass one could see some mountain in the distance forming the backdrop for the farms that lay below. There were few plains for agriculture as we would find in the western United States.

Then there were the mountains! Perhaps with the exception of the mountains of Italy in World War II, U.S. troops had not faced such an array of mountains to be fought over in their many wars around the globe. These were known as the Taebaeks, a veritable array of stratified ranges that occupied the entire eastern half of the Korean Peninsula. Rising high in the sky, this jumbled mass of rocks was to present obstacles to the movement of UN forces throughout the war. The mountains extended from the Yalu River in the north nearly to Pusan on the tip of Korea, and they made movement of men and machines difficult whenever forces moved or deployed in any direction. Only in the narrow valley formed by the Imjin River, which penetrated the spine from Seoul to Wonsan in a southwest-northeast direction, was there any relief from the foreboding heights.

There is simply no way to describe adequately the effect these hills had on the men, summer and winter, or how the fighting might have changed if the men didn't have to overcome the topography as well as the enemy before them. The hardships endured the first year, caused by this massive hump in the eastern region, added substantially to the numbers killed and wounded and changed forever the outcome of the war.

A critical factor in war is the transportation system, and while Korea possessed a rail and road network, it left a lot to be desired. The lack of this network must have placed tremendous challenges on the logistic train, which somehow was able to overcome the problems of getting men, equipment, and supplies to the front and in maintaining the flow of material. It was not working that well at the very beginning of the war. The main roads ran between the principal cities on the general axis of Pusan-Taegu-Taejon-Suwon-Seoul. These were two-lane, hard-surface roads similar to our secondary roads. All other roads were packed gravel or simply trails that meandered through the towns and villages. The roadnet, or in many places the lack thereof, was to have disastrous effects on the UN command later in the year. With the exception of the primary roads, most were extremely dusty in the dry weather and then would turn to mud in the wet weather. I never found any other conditions.

The railroads, which I suspect were built by the Japanese in order to remove their plunder, generally followed the major road-net. Our forces used them to move people and supplies both north and south, depending upon whether we were aggressively attacking or withdrawing to another line.

In addition to the topography, we would find another obstacle – the climate. It was distinctly different from what we had known in Japan. The contrasts between summer and winter weather conditions were considerable. The summer was hot and humid, the only relief being a thundershower, which, though it would cool us for a short time, would also create mud that would make travel far more difficult for both vehicles and men. Fall came early, and as it moved into winter, the cold and humidity combined to make the weather raw. The days would be pleasantly warm, but as the sun descended, the cold penetrated our bodies and we struggled through the night until the sun rose again to give warmth. The contrasts, as might be expected, extended from north to south as well, where the temperature variations were more pronounced. The cyclonic storms we experienced in both the fall and the spring brought more misery to the men, who found little escape from the elements. There were not many times when we were not consciously aware of the weather and its effect on what we were doing.

This, then, was Korea, a land of complexities and historic changes, a place on the map that would change our lives forever. The picture of the country gradually emerging was less than clear; there was still distortions and the blurring of times and events set amid a landscape that was foreign to us in every sense of the word. It was as if the camera was recording scenes out of focus or had been held unsteady.

I was not apprehensive or even scared. I had not been ordered into combat, to attack a hill or to go on patrol, and I was too green and inexperienced at this point to realize what lay ahead. I was uncertain of where I was to be assigned but could assume that I would be joining an infantry unit. I did not know at this time the extremely high mortality rate of infantry platoon leaders, but I would soon learn this awful verity of war. Subconsciously, perhaps, I refused to accept the gravity of my situation or wanted to sweep it under the rug. It was as if my body was a bit in limbo, floating through life disconnected from the brain – or was it the other way around?

Here I was, a young man, who, like thousands of others, could not grasp the enormity of the hour. Was it because we were naive or uninformed or just plain ignorant of what lay before us? No, I believe that we were so self-assured and had so much confidence in "the system" that we did not possess much self-doubt. And our age had some effect on our thinking. Youth believes that it can do anything, take on any challenge, overcome any adversity, and survive in any situation. Now that we had met the country, we were ready to meet the enemy.

That hour was fast approaching. Along the movement route in Japan we had received the news that the United Nations had supported the U.S. resolution to defend South Korea and that other countries were supporting us under the banner of the UN. It was to be a joint effort, the first time that an army would take to the field under this organization. This was pretty heady stuff to hear, but we could not know what it meant. We didn't sit around discussing it very much, but all agreed that it was a good idea to bring troops from other countries into the battle, because it would lend legitimacy to the initial response by U.S. forces. It was great to share the wealth, and there was no end to the speculation and hope that these troops would arrive quickly and we could put an end to the battle. And this was before we left Pusan!

There was tremendous optimism shared by the soldiers. Many believed us to be invincible, and most had little awareness of what lay ahead, of the possibility of being wounded or killed. The men could not or would not accept the impending battle as anything but a skirmish. The American army would make short work of the "gooks." Everyone was already expecting the North Korean army to fold as soon as it met U.S. forces and was confident that we would be back in Japan for Christmas. We had tremendous faith in the ability or luck of the army somehow to mobilize our forces and get them to Korea, so we did not stew over the news. Let's face it, our own experience in getting to Korea should have removed all doubt, but our expectations were that the necessary machinery to put it all in place was already underway.

At the same time, we learned that General MacArthur had been placed in command of UN forces. As supreme commander Allied Powers, Far East Command, he was the "Old Man," the "Chief Honcho," a commander whom we knew as myth rather than a reality. Everyone in Japan in the occupation army had heard of him. He had fought and won the Pacific War, had accepted the Japanese surrender, and had gained many honors in his career as a professional soldier. MacArthur was publicized throughout the command in the *Stars and Stripes,* and that military newspaper was as long on the man as it was on the events surrounding the man. He was highly respected by the Japanese, and he gained their affection easily. In their sight he ranked with the emperor, and the policies he proclaimed were known to all. He was, in fact, a legendary figure. Of course, those of us who had not been assigned to the Tokyo area knew of him through the Armed Forces Radio and the newspapers; none of us had met or known him personally. But it did not surprise us to learn of his appointment, and as a group we were happy that he was in command.

But General MacArthur was still in Japan, and we were in Korea. The wheels were moving, the machine gathering momentum. Pusan had not yet felt the weight of the refugees who were at that moment moving south in great numbers to escape the North Korean army. Even before we left the city, we would see the early arrivals, but they were merely a trickle of what was to become a flood in the near future. As they came, Americans and their allies would be taking the place of the refugees as we headed north. The exchange of refugees for an army was to be profound.

U.S. forces, with their large quantities of supplies and various military equipment, strained the port city to the breaking point. Combat troops and civilian workers milled around the area like ants dislodged from an anthill. The cacophony of men and machines assaulted the ears endlessly, day and night.

We were not put up in barracks or in tent cities; rather, we were allowed to forage for ourselves. Administrators were trying to make sense out of the chaos, but their primary objective was to sort out the transportation problem and to get the men and equipment loaded as quickly as possible. That organization occurred at all is surprising, but it did, and the processing at Pusan improved rapidly. We were directed to a boxcar, or rather we found it ourselves, and made it our temporary home for a few days. It served as our shelter, our cooking shed, and a meeting place.

The American GI has earned a reputation the world over for his generosity and kindness. I saw many of our men sharing their food with hungry, dirty children, and at the time we had little to spare. I became attached to one small, ragged urchin who, with many of his soulmates, was trying to earn a handout shining our dusty boots. (Of course getting our boots shined was about the last thing we wanted.) Kim was perhaps five or six years old. He attached himself to our small group by the boxcar and hung around

My friend Kim with a black officer assigned to the 24th, Pusan, July 1950.
Author's photograph

waiting for some scrap of food or attention. I had a pair of red and
gray pajamas, which had seen better times in Japan, and since
I figured I would not be sacking out in them in Korea, I decided
to cut them down to his size. Finding scissors and thread, I hacked

and sewed and finally got the job done. I told him to find some water and wash himself, and then I gave them to him. He strutted around our campsite like a little peacock. My pictures revive his memory to this day, and I was sad to leave him alone when we moved out.

Originally, my scheduled departure from Japan was July 9. That was the day the first elements of the 25th Infantry Division, to which I was now assigned, landed in Korea and were ordered to Hamchang.

4. First Contact

Ironically, I was now waiting for transportation to the front instead of being aboard a ship sailing to the States. When the train was assembled and ready to depart, I said good-bye to Chaplain Messing and a warrant officer who had made the trip from Japan with me, held young Kim for the last time, and loaded up. Slowly the train left the station. There were few people to wave good-bye. As the train moved from the port area and through the city into the countryside, I got my first glimpse of the land. There were a few factories on the outskirts of Pusan belching black smoke, and there was a sea of wooden houses with tile roofs. Off to our right, the blue-green ocean gleamed in the sun, and on the horizon lay an island.

Again, as in Japan, I was assigned to a boxcar. The rail line paralleled the main highway, but there was little vehicular traffic. The scene was rather peaceful, and there were few people along the route. I do not remember anyone waving us on; unlike the Japanese, who had given us a rousing departure, the Koreans watched us quietly and stoically as we moved past.

On July 13 we arrived at what I believe was the forward command post (CP) of the 24th Infantry Regiment, where I was assigned to the 1st Battalion as a platoon leader of Company A. (See appendix A for a brief history of the 24th Infantry Regiment.) I assume the platoon was already formed when I was given command, but I have no recollection of the events of that day. By the time I left Pusan, Maj. Gen. William F. Dean's 24th Infantry Division had already been pushed back to a line south of Chonan. The situation on all sides was fluid, to say the least. Elements of the 21st Infantry Regiment (Task Force Smith) had made the initial contact south of Suwon on July 5. Since then, they had been fighting, delaying, and withdrawing almost on a daily basis. I knew a brother officer, Lt. Carl Bernard, who had gone through infantry school with me, but at the time I did not know that he had seen combat with the 21st.

Until the 25th Infantry Division arrived in Korea, Dean's com-

Scene from train leaving Pusan, about July 12, 1950. *Author's photograph*

mand had the unenviable job of trying to stop or slow the North Korean advance. It was an impossible task, given the array of opposing forces.

My journal notes are quoted verbatim, and describe rather briefly what followed after my assignment and the days ahead. On July 20 I wrote: "At Sangju. I ran into McCormack. ROK [Republic of Korea] police report fighting in hills NE of town." Sangju was at least a hundred "klicks" (kilometers) northwest of Taegu on the north-south axis, and U.S. forces had already met the enemy. Lieutenant McCormack was another classmate at the infantry school, and upon graduation he, Carl Bernard, and I believe one other officer from our class had been assigned to Japan. I joined the 7th Infantry Division on northern Honshu, while they went south to the 24th Infantry Division. McCormack was going somewhere in a jeep, and I happened to be standing at a crossroads when he drove up and stopped. We greeted each other warmly. His unit had recently been in the fighting and was repositioned somewhere near us. After I took his picture, he sped off. I was never to meet up with him again.

As the 25th Infantry Division moved into position, there were a number of conflicting reports about the actual locations of various units. The 24th Regiment was assigned in the mountainous area north of the Taejon-Taegu road axis to counter the threat of the North Koreans as they moved across the peninsula to get to Taegu. The initial positioning of the regiment was in the vicinity of Kumchon. As was usual in those early days, the regiment was spread out thinly, and all the battalions were on the main line of resistance (MLR). Neither commander of the 24th and 25th infantry divisions had the luxury of reserve forces at his disposal.

This was mountain fighting at its worst. The roadnet was practically nonexistent except for the secondary roads that linked units of the 25th. But the most critical condition was that of getting supplies to the thinly held front. The logistics of meeting the needs was paramount. Units could not sustain effective combat operations without food and ammunition, but even so, the supply train had to contend with the masses of refugees streaming south, clogging the fragile roadnet, as well as remnants of the ROK forces that had caught the brunt of the action and were passing through U.S. lines. Along with refugees and ROKs were the infiltrators, a trained enemy force who changed their clothing and passed through the action areas in order to attack from the rear. The situation was highly charged by the infiltrating forces. Eventually, the Civil Affairs people set up checkpoints to screen these attempts and were able to slow or stop the NKs as they masqueraded as civilians to get behind the lines. The vast numbers of refugees moving south certainly provided cover for the Communists, and many enemy soldiers got through to wreak havoc with rear-echelon troops.

On July 21 I reported: "Battalion moved by rail and motor. Train broke down and was pushed over the hill." (I cannot fathom what the final note means.) When we dismounted, we gathered our equipment and prepared to move out. Our company com-

mander had been given the position coordinates, so we got underway. The order of march was by platoons, so we fell in on the dusty
road and set off in two columns in single file. There was the usual
griping about the army and the damn train and being in the middle of nowhere, the troops thinking they had been short-changed
again.

I often heard, "Someone's always crappin' on us. I don't need
this hassle." Or, "They think we ain't got no feelings." In the lexicon
of the foot soldier the pronoun "they" stands for anyone in authority who has control over the soldier's thoughts or actions. "Those
other ones" include the officers, the noncoms, government officials, the enemy, the train crews, ad infinitum. This time, the men
were venting their anger at the train crew, which had suddenly
dropped them off at some inhospitable place, and now they had
to walk.

As we moved forward, the men started to loosen up a bit and
engaged in some good-natured horseplay, and there was laughter
up and down the line. One thing not yet clear to many of them
was that we were moving into defensive positions to meet and stop
an army and that some of us might not make it through the night.
At the time, no one knew how far apart the two forces were; we
could only speculate that somewhere up ahead we would meet.
The field training exercises, the forced marches, the bivouacs we
had participated in many times in Japan seemed to have little rele-
vance at the moment. Perhaps a few of the officers and noncoms
who had been in action before could grasp the connection, but
for the most part the men moved along oblivious to where they
were going, or what they would find on arrival. In retrospect, this
march probably served a good beginning, for as we would discover
soon enough, it was the first of many such marches in the future.
Within a week, forced marches would become a common occurrence as we withdrew before the North Korean army.

Somewhere along the route we called a halt. We were weary
and hoped to go into bivouac and get some rest. But our time was
running out, so after a short break we kept plodding on.

The next day, July 22, I wrote: "East of Poun. Tactical move
without prior recon. We sight airbursts ahead. Refugees streaming
back. ROKs going to the rear." Normally, reconnaissance is conducted before moving the main force, but we did not have the luxury of time, as we had to get into position as quickly as possible.
I remember that we were not very pleased to see the ROK troops

going to the rear as we moved into defensive positions. There was a lot of grumbling about this from the men; neither they nor I could readily accept the idea that we were going to fight their war. In fact, at this juncture the 25th Infantry Division had been ordered to relieve the ROK 1st and 2d divisions astride and east of the Hamchang-Sangju-Kumchon road and to delay the advance of the North Koreans who were concentrated heavily in that area. But I was not aware of this when we relieved them.

The refugees presented quite a sight. Many soldiers in numerous wars have seen pathetic, homeless refugees moving from a combat area, but this was my first experience with them, and I have to admit that for the most part they were a sorry-looking lot. I felt immediate empathy for them. I was to see them throughout the year in Korea, moving with the tides of war, and the sight and sound of them is as vivid today as when it happened. They had come out of Seoul or Suwon or from half a dozen places, fleeing south with all their worldly goods. Fear, or the pain of leaving home, was etched across each face and lent impetus to the flight from the Communist invaders. A few pushed their possessions in makeshift carts, and here and there an ox-drawn wagon carried goods piled high, but most carried their belongings on A-frames strapped to their backs.

On July 23 I wrote: "Early movement forward. This is an extended move. Miles covered unknown. Twisting roads. Alert for enemy. Arrival first village. Captain Lew predicts enemy mortar fire. Movement again. Pass through 17th ROK Division. Pick up one officer and ten ROKs. Proceed to set up defense covering broad valley. Observation good." I assume that the ROK soldiers were to lead us into the defensive positions. This was our first contact with South Korean soldiers. They were commanded by a Captain Lew, who appeared to be about my age, and he and I became friends rather quickly. I know that he stayed with us for a few days in the defensive area, and after we had gotten settled in, we had plenty of time to talk. He knew precious little about the enemy intentions, but certainly more than we did. Since he spoke English rather well, I was able to pick his brains about the situation that was quickly developing to our front. He was helpful, I recall, in positioning both men and heavy weapons. I had learned how to set up a defense, both in the classroom and in field exercises, but this one was for real, and I would not have some instructor critiquing me on where I had gone wrong. Lew was a bright officer and made kind sugges-

Korean refugees pour out of a village near Yongdok headed south, July 29, 1950. *U.S. Army photograph*

tions to me, since he was not in command. More important, because of his culture, and in deference to me, it would have been wrong for him to take charge.

I had a camera with me that I had brought from Japan and snapped a few pictures of the first location, the placement of heavy machine guns, and the troops in position on the hill. The pictures reveal that we were situated below the crest of the hill on the forward slope facing a broad valley in which was located the town of Poun. As soon as we settled in, I sketched the 1st Battalion's positions. It was the first and last time that I bothered. Yet I can still recall many of the defensive positions I established. Starting almost immediately, North Korean patrols attempted to identify our defenses and to probe for weak points along the line. In our immediate area, things were quiet, but I believe C Company felt the initial probing actions.

The same was not true for sister units of the 24th. Three days before, they had fought their way into the town of Yechon in a limited offensive action against the North Koreans. On the first day the enemy could not be dislodged, so the attacking units withdrew for the night before going on the attack the following morning. This action was successful, and after some fighting, the units occupied the town. This was the first city recaptured by American troops, and the success of the battle gave the rest of us a much-needed morale lift. While not a major battle, it was a symbolic victory for U.S. ground troops and was so reported in the *Congressional Record* shortly thereafter.

On July 24 I noted: "First patrol action to Poun. Enemy sighted. 57-mm fieldpiece captured by patrol. Mission to reconnoiter high ground and observe road and railnet from Chung-ju to Taejon. Signal for return: flicker jeep lights three times." This was my first reconnaissance patrol, and I received specific instructions about the mission. I was not to get engaged in a firefight, and if we were fired upon, I was to withdraw. I am certain that I was apprehensive about the order but accepted it as something that had to be done. By this time we knew that Seoul had been captured and that the North Koreans were moving swiftly to the south and Taejon. At that time the NKs were staging in the Poun valley, and our commanders wanted to know what was ahead of them. We had been given a mission. The regiment was to fight a delaying action along the Hamchang-Yongdok road. The 1st Battalion was located still forward, and I believe its initial position was about ninety miles from Seoul. The town of Poun lay in a wide valley and was about twenty miles northeast of Taejon.

Since I had taken the patrol to within two miles of Poun, I claimed that we had gotten about eighty-two miles from Seoul on the mission. I cannot substantiate this claim, but we did return with our first war trophy, a 57-mm field gun. It was of Russian manufacture. It was an unusually long, crudely made, hand-carried weapon that had been abandoned along the way. After reaching the high ground overlooking the town, we stayed in position observing the roadnet for several hours. Troops were moving in and out of the area, but we were too distant to identify the units or their strength. We returned to our lines, and I reported the patrol action.

The next day I wrote: "Third Battalion to our right rear makes contact. Savage fighting followed." By this time all units were in position and had dug in, and we were waiting for the North Koreans to strike. They bypassed our position, and the 3d Battalion caught the major force of the attack. I believe that on the same day I took photographs that show the deployment of our positions, but then the camera failed, so I threw it down the hill into some brush after removing the film. Then we waited for another probing action.

On July 26 I reported: "Begin withdrawal S. Company B under command Captain Hash counterattacks through I Company. Secures hill at dusk. Organized withdrawal took place while General Wilson, Major Carson, and I waited." Because of enemy strength and determination, headquarters had ordered this withdrawal. Until this time, as far as I know, withdrawals had been disorganized. I think this was the first of many withdrawals, because my notes were made at the time. However, it may have been several days later. What is clear is that the three of us were at a dark and lonely intersection in the middle of nowhere as elements of the regiment passed through to the rear. I cannot postulate how I was separated from the platoon, or the circumstances that placed me at the crossroads with General Wilson, the assistant division commander (ADC), and Major Carson, my battalion commander. General Wilson was a tough, reliable soldier, and at some point along the way assisted in the ever-increasing number of withdrawals that took place. As the units moved past us, they were very quiet, and the dull shuffling sound of boots hitting the gravel and the noises made by the personal equipment carried wearily along by the soldiers exaggerated the loneliness of that outpost. The rapidly changing tactical situation forced us to readjust and reorganize on a regular schedule, then to set up some new defensive position to hold for another day before withdrawing again at night. I do not remember my unit counterattacking in order to give relief to a sister unit and allow it to extricate from a critical spot, but we may have done so. I do know that fear was clearly written across the faces of the men, during the day as we waited for an attack, or at night when we left a position to move south.

Fear was palpable, it registered on the senses, it changed in degree but was ever-present. Personal fear is something that most men face in combat. It is the fear of being wounded or killed or lost from one's unit. There is no shame in being afraid, and while men rarely will admit to it, it lurks in the recesses of the mind until a dangerous situation occurs, and then it surfaces to taunt the person. Fear can be rational, I believe, or irrational, and certain fears can be transmitted from one to another. It can permeate a group of men in a horrifying way, even in the same unit, while those further removed from the scene will not be afflicted at all. I cannot recall a single man who did not face it or experience fright to some extent during the fighting. I believe there are soldiers who are able to overcome fear, even when the terror of the unknown that lay before them caused lesser men to shrink openly from the job at hand.

When fear becomes paramount and one cannot face it or accept it as a natural reaction of all animals, then that emotion can paralyze the soldier and he ceases to be a functioning part of the unit. Fear, or the conditions that beget fear, is prevalent throughout a battle zone, but we must learn to cope with it.

In any case, the general, the major, and I stood there watching the men pass through. There was little talk; from time to time, one of the gunners (I believe they were military police) would want relief from his position on the jeep, and someone else would replace him behind the machine gun mounted on one of the two trucks. They were the ADC's "shotguns," or guard detail.

On July 27, "New defensive positions controlling roadnet [were] set up." Exactly where this occurred is questionable, but since we had been playing a game of leapfrog the day before, it was probably south and east of our previous position. The tactics went something like this: one unit would withdraw and set up a defensive position, and then another would withdraw through the first and establish its own position. Then that unit would hold the line as the first unit passed through it. This worked well until one of the units was attacked, or until it was flanked by the enemy. Then a counterattack was ordered to try to straighten the line. The real problem was that it was extremely difficult for the commanders to know precisely where the lines were or where gaps in the line had been penetrated. The enemy forces took advantage of every move we made and knew where the open space between units lay. All along this line the pressure kept increasing. We received mortar fire, but the enemy's focus was on our sister battalion, which received heavy firepower and was forced to withdraw from some areas.

I wrote on July 28: "Battalion counterattacks high ground to our front." This action resulted in relieving pressure on the second battalion, but then we were attacked in turn. We held across the line, and the enemy withdrew. In our sector, things were relatively quiet, and we had a chance to lick our wounds and wait for the next probing attacks. They came quickly, and all along the line while it was still daylight the North Koreans started moving forward. At this time of the war, I had yet to receive barbed wire or any special

defensive material: We had no flares or antipersonnel mines or anything available to help repel an enemy attack. For the most part,
we were a holding force sent into position to attempt to hold real
estate, but even if we had been sent some of these items, we were
never in place long enough to set them up.

One of the lessons learned early on was that our training methods and our fighting skills had to be modified in Korea. Inexperienced combat officers, certainly those with the training of a rifle
platoon leader, were initially at a distinct disadvantage when it came
to meeting the enemy. We went into position, established fields
of fire, attempted to determine the likeliest approach routes, and
then waited for the attack. We were familiar with flanking maneuvers, how to defend, when to mount counterattacks, and when
to withdraw. The training at the infantry school at Fort Benning
emphasized the classical configuration of an infantry unit on the
MLR, supported by artillery and armor, but it did not stress night
fighting, guerrilla tactics, or mass attacks such as those we encountered in those first weeks.

The land itself was of primary importance to us, and I found
myself examining every topographical feature critically. After forty
years I can, without resort to pictures, conjure up a particular piece
of real estate where sole action took place. I can visualize all over
again the mountains and the plains, the rivers and the valleys, the
rice terraces and the fields of grain, and the depleted hills rising
over them. The land features were important because fighting a
ground war requires one to look for advantages in the terrain, and
then to use them effectively to stop the enemy, attack them, or
to hold them in place. All infantry officers learn the importance
of capturing and holding the high ground and during a battle must
know the best approach route to take during the attack, which offers
the best protection from observation and fire, and how to assess
the land being held by an enemy. When I traveled in a vehicle,
I constantly surveyed the route we were taking. Where was the
best spot for an ambush? How could I react if we were hit? What
side of the road offered the best defense? Was there a way out
of the trouble spot?

We were not trained to be geographers, but we certainly were
educated in using a map, reading map coordinates, identifying
topographical features, and analyzing the terrain over which we
were fighting. We lived by our maps (when available) as readily
and as easily as we ate or slept in Korea. We plotted our advances
and our withdrawals; we learned our objectives as map references

rather than a specific town or city or river or bridge. We identified the enemy's location on the maps and their avenues of attack, and the gaps between units on the MLR. Maps offered us a direction without which we could not have fought in a strange land, or even known how to begin. They were invaluable in combat; without them we were lost.

I knew that the high ground provided the best place to gain or hold a military advantage over the enemy, and to gain such an advantage I had to lead the men into battle, or on patrol, and my platoon had to use firepower to kill the enemy. One of the classical maneuvers we had studied was to use both artillery and tanks to recapture a lost position, to counterattack as expeditiously as we could organize, and to dig in as soon as we reached our objective. There was never any second-guessing in the platoon; no one ever questioned my authority or the orders I issued. Perhaps I had an advantage. I joined the platoon at the outset of the war, moved into the first defensive position with it, selected the men, and went on the first patrol action.

In the early days of the war, when we stayed in defensive positions only long enough to repel the enemy before moving to another line, it became clear that we had to learn new rules of engagement. The enemy outnumbered us significantly and fought tough and mean, using tactics that had little similarity to what we had learned. The North Koreans would attack en masse along the front, striking a particular position, and if they could not take the objective, their forces would flow around the ends and attack from the flanks. Since we were numerically outnumbered and outgunned, and since we rarely had friendly forces on line to protect our flanks, the maneuver frequently was successful against us. The "long gray line" was stretched to the breaking point, and it never was long enough. Not until we withdrew to the Pusan Perimeter were we able to go into the classical stance of placing units on line.

I could easily understand the logic of making successive withdrawals. It gave us the chance to reorganize a bit, however briefly, set up new positions to halt the enemy, and fight the battle with the minimum number of casualties. As we moved backward, our defensive positions were tenuous at best. They were nothing more than holding actions. We had little in the way of defensive equipment to help us set up a reinforced position, nor did we possess adequate reserve units to give us depth. We were generally isolated in some location for such short periods that it was difficult to establish artillery concentrations or other direct fire support on a suspected enemy avenue of approach. While we might have had some interdiction artillery fire in front of us, I cannot remember much of any in those early days. Neither can I remember the use of artillery illuminating rounds, but perhaps there was more cannon action than I recall.

Of the various support units that provided assistance throughout the Korean campaign, the one that I called upon most frequently was the 159th Field Artillery Battalion. They were a well-trained unit, and the firepower they brought on the NKs frequently made the difference in the action underway. How many times they were able to persuade the enemy troops to back off, or to give it up completely, I do not know. This unit was also black, and during the times I used it to provide support, it was never lacking. The battalion had one of the best records of the many units in Korea. On more than one occasion, when frontline positions were overrun and the NKs had penetrated into the rear areas, a shootout would occur. The artillerymen simply lowered the tubes and fired point-blank into the enemy forces. There were instances when I called for support that could not be provided at the moment, but usually the gunners were waiting to assist whenever they could. The forward observers (FOs) who were attached to the line companies were a great moral boost. They lived with us, and frequently their attention to the battle provided the difference between victory or defeat. Division artillery was equipped with heavier cannons, 155-mm howitzers, which could reach out much further, and they were in use nearly as much as the direct support battalions.

While we had artillery support for indirect fire and tankers who could give us direct fire on NK positions, the fact of the matter was that we had to depend on the equipment and weapons that were organic to the battalion. This was certainly true at the outset of the fighting. Most of the weapons and communications equipment was of World War II vintage. Some officers carried the Colt .45, but generally we carried .30-caliber carbines, while most of the men had M1 rifles. If memory serves me, each squad was equipped with a Browning automatic rifle (BAR), but it may have been issued only to the weapons squad. These squads also had a .30-caliber light or heavy machine gun. The lights were air cooled and the heavies were water cooled, but it is hard to say which was preferred. I know that when we deployed for the first time, we had at least one heavy MG in position.

Both 60-mm and 81-mm mortars were assigned for support, the 60s at the platoon level, and the 81s as part of the Weapons

Platoon. This platoon also had two relatively new weapons: the 57-mm and the 75-mm recoilless rifles. Both had entered the army's inventory after having been field-tested during World War II. They were powerful direct-fire pieces that propelled with great accuracy various types of ammo, including high explosive antitank (HEAT), high explosive(HE), and white phosphorus (WP). They were a welcome addition to the fighting. We also had the 2.36-inch rocket launchers to use against tanks or armored vehicles, but since we spent most of our time in the hills, they were not used much. One of the most effective weapons was the fragmentation grenade, universally carried by the troops. It was lethal, and I for one felt a bit naked when I did not have several strapped to my body. From time to time we would pick up some smoke grenades, but we did not carry them generally. Early on, wanting to have more ammunition available on my person, I taped two thirty-round "banana" clips for my carbine end-to-end, which gave me sixty rounds ready in place. The straight magazines for the carbine held only fifteen rounds each, and I was able to slide the canvas pouch holding two clips onto the stock of the carbine. Thus I always had ninety rounds of ammo with the weapon, whatever happened.

From time to time other weapons were picked up. Some men carried the .45-caliber Thompson MG and the .45-caliber submachine gun. We called the latter a grease gun, since it resembled one. It packed a tremendous wallop, but because of the recoil from the escaping gases and its short barrel, it lacked any great accuracy. None of my men were equipped with either of these two weapons, however. I once witnessed the power of a .45 slug when the bullet hit a man in the wrist, and it spun the poor unfortunate soul around like a top. Several times I saw weapons that had been plucked from a dead NK soldier, but I would not allow the men to fire the weapons when we were in position. The NK burp gun, a rapid-fire submachine gun sporting a cylindrical magazine, was a desirable souvenir, but its unique sound when fired caused a bit of consternation among the troops. On balance, while there was some skepticism about some of our weapons, they were certainly on a par with those used by the North Koreans. In most cases they were superior and provided us with good firing capabilities.

Another thought became of paramount importance to me at that time. The North Koreans' effective tactics of applying pressure along the so-called MLR, and their repeated breakthroughs suddenly made me aware of our vulnerability. Although I never heard the word "retreat" used by anyone, it was almost a foregone conclusion that any position we occupied would have to be abandoned and we would be ordered to fall back again.

Sometime during the first withdrawals the men lost their sense of superiority. There came a sudden recognition that the enemy was tough and well trained. We had been tested in a few short days and nights, and already there were some who had lost their enthusiasm for a fight and could only hope for reinforcements to arrive to help. I believed the army was doing everything possible to provide support, but I was realistic enough to understand the logistics problem that it faced. After all, I had experienced enough of the road and rail systems going up from Pusan and was convinced that the movement of supplies and soldiers was a horrendous task for the rear-echelon people.

The men in the platoon did not share my optimism that help would eventually arrive, and they remained unhappy with the moves from one position to another. They were also frustrated with the lack of support (both in terms of people and supplies), and it was a major job to continue to rally any enthusiasm for the tasks at hand.

When we attacked and had won a position, the men were so exhausted that all they wanted to do was lie down on top of the hill and rest. I do not think that we were physically soft (although we would harden our bodies in short order); rather, the endless round of fighting and falling back and counterattacking was already starting to take its toll.

About this time, we got the clear, unequivocal word that General Walker, commanding general (CG) of the U.S. Eighth Army, had ordered us to stand and fight. We were to die in this Godforsaken place, a country to which we had only recently been sent, and the news was disturbing to each of us. We had not been slackers in any sense of the word. We were tired and hungry and scared. Each day had been a nightmare, and we resented the message that came forward. Every man had seen the enemy close up, and that enemy's relentless, rolling attacks and ability to infiltrate through the lines and attack from the rear or the flank were unnerving, to say the least. Walker's message to his staff was succinct:

> There will be no retreating, withdrawal or adjustment of the lines, or any other term you may choose. There is no line behind us to which we can retreat. Every unit must counterattack to keep the enemy in confusion and off balance.
>
> There will be no Dunkirk; there will be no Bataan. A retreat to Pusan would be one of the greatest butcheries in history. We must

fight to the end. Capture by these people is worse than death itself.

We will fight as a team. If some of us must die, we will die fighting together. Any man who gives ground may be responsible for the death of thousands of his comrades.

I want you to put this out to all the men in the divisions. I want everybody to understand we are going to hold this line. We are going to win!

Notwithstanding the order, and considering the deteriorating situation, a general withdrawal was already in the wind, and it arrived shortly thereafter.

One other incident occurred before the move. I remember that one afternoon, before it got dark, we spotted two men walking down one of the dirt roads in full view. At that time, the South Koreans had pretty well disappeared, and I thought it strange to see anyone at all. I sent a squad to investigate the pair. North Korean soldiers had, we learned quickly, been issued the ubiquitous white clothing of Korea, and when they or their commanders thought it necessary, they would switch clothes or drape their civilian dress over the uniform. As they got within sight, the two North Koreans saw the squad and took off running. The men started firing and killed both of them.

In spite of General Walker's order, on July 31 I could write: "General withdrawal. Regiment gave me orders: 'Commence at dark and not later than 2130 hours.'" I am sure the orders came from battalion to the company and then to me; that is the normal chain of command. The statement appears a bit officious, but that is what is recorded in my notes. "Began road march 6 miles west of Sangju. Passed through Sangju; continued through valley for 9 [miles] more. Refugees were leaving. Roads were jammed with everything they owned – cattle, carts, bicycles." Until the withdrawal order, we were still fighting a delaying action along the Hamchang-Yongdok road. At the same time, most of the division had moved south to counter the enemy forces, which were expected to attack east to Pusan, but we were unaware of this as we stayed in position. This tactical move was necessary to gain the time necessary to relocate the larger force in the vicinity of Chinju. Then we broke contact with the North Korean army and began a withdrawal to the south.

My notes reveal the frustration of retreating. "It was hard for us to give up ground. Even the men sensed that it was all wrong. Our doctrine on defense was to stop the enemy, repel his charges, and if he was successful in penetrating our defenses, to counterattack with reserves. But can anyone follow these principles if his reserves are limited or nonexistent? So, the North Korean army continued to push, probing for some weakness here or there along our lines. Eventually, the end of the line would be reached, our flanks would be exposed, and we would withdraw again. It was an altogether different type of fighting, as we were forced to withdraw to the rear."

On August 1 I wrote: "0645 hours. Stumble wearily into assembly area. The mountain faced us." Again, I do not remember what is meant exactly by this note. Perhaps our exhaustion made the mountain looming before us formidable, but this is only a supposition. The previous day had been long and tiring, and we had moved generally south and to the east, holding successive defensive positions, for at least a week. Whether this was the assembly area along the Taejon-Taegu road axis or further south, I do not know. I remember that we marched for what seemed hours before we stopped. Somewhere along our withdrawal route we were picked up in vehicles and transported south to Chinju or the Masan area for deployment again.

As we were getting ready to leave on the night of July 31, I ran into a Captain ———, who was our battalion medical officer. Noting my near-exhaustion, he offered me a pep pill, with the admonition that it would keep me on a high for twenty-four hours, after which time I "would probably fall dead on my feet." I don't know what it was, but I sailed along fine until we got to the assembly area. I bedded the platoon, found myself a place to rest, and promptly fell asleep. Whether it was the pill or just the emotional release of being off the line, I don't know, but it was a glorious sleep.

While we were still west of Sangju, attempting to delay the enemy's timetable, and unknown to us at the time, a strong, well-equipped North Korean force was racing south over the plains of western Korea, from where it intended to sweep east to the critical port of Pusan. Since there was little opposition to its movement, the army barreled toward the objective. This strategic move was an obvious threat that had to be countered at any cost, for the loss of the port facilities would have been a disaster for the UN forces.

As the spearheading elements of the North Korean army with support forces moved south, U.S. troops continued to blast the tank forces and the infantry's frontal attacks, but on July 20, after a running tank-infantry battle, U.S. forces withdrew from the Taejon area and headed southeast. There have been numerous accounts of the battle of Taejon, and the fact is that U.S. units fought the NKs street by street and finally were forced to abandon the city. By this time the 25th Infantry had withdrawn to a new line placed between Taejon to our west and Taegu on the south. Then the division was ordered to stop the other NK threat, which was sweeping across the southern tip of Korea from the west toward Pusan. It was this enemy action that had precipitated our general withdrawal on July 31.

Looking back on that period, I believe that U.S. forces fought well. That we were forced to withdraw must be attributed to the continuous infiltration and flanking tactics used by a numerically superior force. The North Korean army was well trained and aggressive, its supplies more than adequate, its tactics well planned and executed. The enemy was on a roll that would not end until they reached the Pusan Perimeter.

In the assembly area we received our first news from home and read the news releases or clippings sent with the letters. Information up to this time had been scant, and for most of the month we had no news at all. Rumors abounded, but they were just that. There was a lot of adverse criticism about the fighting ability of the American soldier. Some articles portrayed us as being "soft," stating that the occupation army was "weak and flabby," that "citizen-soldiers" don't possess the willingness to fight. (Even today, the same refrain can be read.) This was total nonsense.

The training programs instituted in the Far East Command under General MacArthur were constant, well organized, and well executed. We participated in small-unit training, starting from the squad up, as well as battalion training exercises. In northern Honshu my regiment spent a lot of time in the field in all kinds of weather, running through tactical maneuvers in the hills and fields of Japan. Specialist training was provided; units were sent off to train in amphibious landings. I doubt if there was anyone who did not believe he was being readied for future combat, and the training was rigorous and constructive. In our home garrison, we rotated troops in and out of the field training exercises; there was a lot of bitching and complaining, but we followed orders.

We read the reports and resented the accusations. For the most part we were green and untested, and with the exception of the noncoms and the more senior officers, most had not experienced combat before. In those early days there were many of us, black and white alike, who were young and innocent, who had never seen death or dying, and who were afraid of it. Yet for all that, we fought a strange war right from the outset, a filthy war of formidable mountains and scarred ridges, of twisting trails, of hunger and disease and heat. Only those who had fought a hidden, crafty opponent or heard the thump of mortars or the whine of artillery shells could understand how we felt about these misrepresentations of the truth. We knew our weaknesses, but they could not be attributed to the so-called easy life in Japan.

What the news articles failed to mention or report was the fact that an austerity program had been imposed by the U.S. Congress on the Department of Defense, the net effect of which was a reduction in equipment and supplies for the Far East Command. The U.S. forces in Japan got a lot less than was needed.

Notwithstanding the criticism, I believe the soldiers and sailors and airmen acquitted themselves superbly in those first critical weeks. The men were as good as, if not better than, any force at any time. There were times when we had little to eat and no change of clothing for months on end, when we had neither ponchos or blankets or were short on ammunition and water and slaked our thirst in insect-infested rice paddies. I remember when a gallon can of corned-beef hash and another of peaches were the only food the platoon had all day, and other days when we had nothing at all. Coupled with our advances and our withdrawals was our sense of frustration at having to give up ground. We gained a quick lesson in humility as the hordes came against us. We learned to modify the classical infantry tactics that we had learned at Fort Riley and Fort Benning and that we used in Japan. This enemy was wily and brave and quite willing to die. I believe that we fought well at times, holding onto a critical position, but the enemy's advantages of superior numbers, short supply lines, mountain tactics, and guerrilla warfare caused us much confusion and despair in those early days. We fought the enemy on strange ground, while they fought over terrain on which they had been scratching out a living their entire life. It is not difficult to understand the opposing positions, and rather quickly we stopped questioning the enemy's ability to fight us.

Several authors have written completely untrue accounts of the 24th Infantry and have insinuated that soldiers of the regiment had "bugout fever," the urge to run or withdraw in the face of overwhelming forces. They have also perpetrated the nonsense that members of the 24th sat around campfires singing the "Bugout Boogie" Max Hastings wrote in his book *The Korean War* that "on July 20 the 24th Infantry of 25th Division broke and fled after their first few hours in battle at Yechon. The pattern of the 24th's first action was repeated in the days that followed. . . . It became necessary to set up roadblocks behind the 24th's positions, to halt deserters and stragglers leaving the lines." What he failed to report was that ROK troops evacuated the town and elements of the regiment were ordered to retake the town. The unit was unsuccessful the first day, but at dawn the following day it attacked and finally drove the North Koreans from their positions in the town.

Early in the war, Marguerite Higgins, a respected war correspondent, wrote of the despair shared by many young soldiers as they faced devastating human waves of North Koreans that poured against them. While this comment has been attributed to the 24th Regiment, in fact, she wrote about the 24th Infantry Division before the 25th Infantry Division arrived in Korea. General Dean, who commanded the 24th Division until his capture, made reference in his book *General Dean's Story* to his troops "bugging out" as early as July 8.

The fact that troops "bugged out" cannot be denied, but in my judgment the soldiers of all units early in the war had that propensity. The men of the 24th Regiment performed no better and no worse than those of other units, and it is unfair to judge them otherwise because they were black. It is ludicrous to suggest that troops sang around a campfire, and even more that roadblocks had to be established. There was never a time when my troops left a position without an order to withdraw.

5. The Pusan Perimeter

The first few days of August were a time for reorganizing and re-placing equipment and also provided a short rest while we waited for orders. The North Korean army had not been idle. They had been delayed in their end-run operation to reach Pusan, but pressure mounted on what would soon become known as the Pusan Perimeter. Our breather lasted only a short time. Fresh troops had begun arriving in Korea, and the United Nations command had decided to pull back to defensive positions inside the Naktong River. As part of the plan, the 25th Infantry Division was ordered to move south, and by August 2–3 it had taken up positions on the left, or south, flank of the UN line in the vicinity of Masan.

The most direct approach to Pusan was the Chinju-Masan route, which was where the North Koreans had concentrated their forces in order to break through to Pusan. Pressure from these troops continued, even though the division had been able to slow the advance in the Chinju area. By this time, the 25th had started to receive some additional units that had arrived in Pusan. Among these were two infantry battalions and a heavy tank battalion. They could not have come at a better time; it enabled the division to strengthen its position between the ocean on the most southern flank and the Naktong River, about fifteen miles northwest of Masan.

There was still some doubt, I believe, about our ability to stop the North Korean charge down the direct approach corridor. I remember clearly that some officers had prepared an escape kit, which they carried with them in the event we had to evacuate by way of the water. Some carried old gas-mask bags, the contents of which had been abandoned along the way, and used the container to carry a few critical items. From several high points we could see the ocean in the far distance, and because of the many withdrawals we had made during the previous month, there was a mentality of defeat and a dreadful sense of foreboding. Fortunately, this was quickly overcome once we started to stand and fight on the perimeter.

Our days of running were about over. We went into an attack

mode on August 6 and continued for the next three days. There was continuous shifting of attack forces and pressure being applied by the North Koreans along the front. Intelligence reports coming in were sketchy at best, and the lines fluctuated and changed even before the news was confirmed. As a platoon leader, my immediate concern was which units were on my left and right, and what kind of firepower support I could expect from them and the artillery in an indirect fire-support role. Much of the information received was either fragmented or exaggerated, but to the best of its ability the battalion staff was trying to keep us informed. During this time we moved, shifted, attacked, fell back, and attacked again.

On August 9, a large North Korean force hit the defensive positions in our area. It was around 1300 hours, and the sun was at its zenith. I do not recall whether the enemy broke through, but two infantry companies were committed abreast to attack these forces, while the third company was directed to flank the position and attack the enemy from the rear. In other words, this would be a classic pincer movement, with only one-half of the pincer.

The fighting was long and costly. As the afternoon wore on, we were forced to give up the ground we had just fought for. We could not hold it without mortar or artillery support, and there was none available. We fell back into still another defensive position as daylight slid into darkness. We did not know it at the time, but we would not fight over the same ground for another six weeks, and then only after we had jumped off the perimeter in a major attack along the entire line. Company platoons were then assigned areas to hold for the night. I had only a few soldiers left, the others having been killed or wounded during the fight, and I was not happy with the prospects of still another attack with so few men.

The first thing I did was to set up a perimeter defense, pull the troop as close together as possible, and pray that we would make it through the night. It was almost too dark to lay out fields of fire or to do much beyond arranging for supporting fire within the hastily set perimeter. I called the men together and briefed them as follows: "OK, we're all pretty pooped, so you don't have to dig in unless you want to. We may or may not get hit tonight, so I want you to stay awake or take turns sleeping. I want one person to be on guard while the other sleeps. Sergeant Nollie and I will be checking on you through the night. I expect that we'll get it in the morning, so be alert as soon as the sun starts coming up. Any questions?"

"Yeah, Lieutenant," one man answered. "I don't have much ammunition."

"So what the hell did you do with it?" I asked. Turning to Sergeant Nollie, I said, "Sergeant, see what you can scrounge up from the others and give this dick some."

I was getting mad. "No damned good reason for you not having the ammo! What the hell did you do with it? You just got tired of lugging it along. Now get your ass out of here and find your hole. You better pray to God that we don't get hit tonight, or your ass is mud!"

There were no more questions. The men wandered off to their assigned places, and the hill got quiet as the night closed in on us. Sergeant Nollie and I sat behind the rocks and tried to talk. I wasn't too happy with the state of things, and the shortage of ammunition concerned me. I probably had reacted too harshly, but then I was responsible for this unit, and it weighed heavily upon me.

I told Nollie how proud I was of the platoon, including that clown who dropped his ammo (I was absolutely convinced that he had shed the slings on our way up). I said I thought they had done a hell of a job the last three days. We also talked about one of the men who had been killed, and the fact that a few artillery rounds might have made a difference.

Nollie commented that we needed more men in a hurry. If we had to sit there, we had to have some kind of a defense set up. I agreed; I already had requested replacements as well as ammunition, wire, flares, and some antipersonnel mines. I told Nollie to get the men moving in the morning as soon as they had eaten. "Got to get holes dug and some wire in place."

Normally, setting up a defense calls for digging in, stringing barbed wire, and setting trip flares and antipersonnel mines to slow down the enemy. The theory is that they will get hung up in the wire, which allows the defense to lay down a withering field of fire to stop them. It generally does slow down enemy soldiers for a while but does not necessarily stop them. Since we did not have any wire or flares or mines, we would have to wait until some were carried up the hill.

Nollie shared my concern. He knew as well as I did the precarious position we were in. "Let's just hope to God that we have a quiet night," he said. Then he left to check each of the positions before he sacked out and to tell the men to get back on the reverse side of the hill in the morning before first light. We did not want them to give away our position. When he returned after making the rounds he reported that all were tired but awake, and he had passed on my orders.

In all the time we had been together, I had not really had the chance to size this man up, but in the last few days I had discovered that he was a special person and would become an even more special friend. Sergeant Nollie was Regular Army, and it showed in everything he did. I regret to say that I don't remember his first name; from the time I met him, he was Sergeant Nollie to me, and I was Lieutenant to him. I remember him as being a bit shy of six feet, with a slight barrel chest. He had a strong face, but it reflected a gentleness that I did not often see in men. His eyes were warm, and his voice was rather soft; I rarely saw him angry and never spiteful or vindictive. He was good natured, but he did not smile often. In many ways he was a serious soldier doing a serious duty, and it was only occasionally that he opened up and talked of Japan or the girl he left behind.

Earlier, when I was assigned to the company and had been given the platoon, Sergeant Nollie was the first man I met. He had trained with the platoon in Japan and knew most of the men, and they responded to him well. I can only speculate about what the men thought when I arrived, but Sergeant Nollie, in his infinite wisdom, let the men know that I was the platoon leader. Because they respected him and his ability, they respected me. From the initial meeting until I left the platoon, there wasn't a man who questioned my right to command or who refused to pay me respect, and I believe it was because of Nollie's leadership, a fact that would be demonstrated time and again in the months ahead. He was the consummate noncom; I couldn't have asked for any better. He was indispensable, and I loved the man.

When we finally got into position on top of the hill (soon dubbed the Rock), I found two large boulders forming a rough L, which I decided would be the platoon CP. They were located on the military crest (the point on the hill where the enemy's observation is the most limited, or slightly on the reverse slope). The forward one was about five feet in height, and the side to the rear was formed almost vertical to the ground. On its left, facing the forward slope, was another stone nearly as high, at a right angle to the first. About two feet from the point of convergence a small tree was growing, and it offered concealment and some sparse shade when the sun boiled down on us. The boulders gave us shelter from incoming rounds and even acted as a solar collector during the hot day to give us a bit of warmth at night. Because of the configuration of the stones, there was room for one man to lie down while the other stood a few feet away. Sergeant Nollie and I established a watch, during which I slept from about nine to one in the morning, at which time he would awake me, and we exchanged places. I considered it to be a perfect position, and it would remain the focal point of the platoon in the days following.

This insignificant piece of land in the Taebaeks would form a small part of the line called the Pusan Perimeter. For the next month it was to be our home. My recollection is that when we went into position, the 1st Battalion was on the left in the regimental sector, while the 2d and 3d battalions occupied the right-flank areas. My guess is that all units were on line and none in reserve. The 24th went into defensive positions near the town of Haman in the sector that included Hill 665, or Battle Mountain, as it would soon be called. It was the focal point on which the army records of the Korean War would indict the regiment for having "mass hysteria," "fleeing before the enemy," "rampant desertion," and "failure to obey orders issued by white officers." The regiment was vilified in the press as the "Bugout Brigade" and the "Running 24th." The truth of the matter is that while some men and units did vacate or were forced from defensive positions in August and did indeed prove themselves to be less than trustworthy, the bulk of the men fought well. The casualty lists for the period were high, and it was a disgrace and disservice to indict the entire regiment unfairly in such a way.

The greater line extended from the sea at Masan north through the 24th Infantry Division then to the 1st Cavalry Division west of Taegu, where it abruptly curved to the north and then east to Tungdok. The perimeter on the north was defended by ROK divisions which covered the area to the coast. While this defensive line appeared to be strong, in fact we were strung out, and the line was thinly held. As a result, swift, mobile forces had to be shifted along the line frequently to fight "brush fires" when the enemy broke through the line or were preparing a major force. Often when these incidents occurred, the 27th Infantry, a sister regiment, was called upon to contain the action, and its soldiers quickly earned the name "firemen."

Now that we were in place, I was told to sit tight. I don't know what this order meant, since for all practical purposes, I had about one squad of men left and there wasn't much we could do except sit. In those days a full platoon had close to forty men; my notes indicate that I went into position with nine. In any case, I had a skeleton of what had been a larger body, so before turning in, I requested replacements. I was not very pleased with my situation. We could not see our flank troops, and my concern was that an attacking force would probe along the line and then hit the space between units. This had been the pattern before, and I saw no reason that it would not continue. Reserve units for backup and support were scarce. On at least two occasions my platoon was withdrawn from the line but just as quickly was placed in another position. This tactic (consistent with the old army joke "two up and one back, and feed 'em a hot meal") was a luxury Eighth Army could ill afford to practice. In the triangular organization of an infantry division, two companies, two battalions, or two regiments were placed on the MLR, while the third corresponding unit would remain in reserve. There was no way for that to happen at this time. So we sat on the Rock and waited for new orders.

The first night I was very apprehensive; as exhausted as I was, I could not sleep. I had an overwhelming and unshakable sense that, come morning, we would be hit. I was right. At dawn, the North Koreans attacked. To my immediate left, one of our machine guns commenced its staccato chatter. Soon other weapons began a chant, returning the fire, and the battle was joined. To our right front, where just a few hours ago we had tried to dislodge the enemy, we saw them moving into attack formation. Through my binoculars, little brown figures were moving forward, evidently determined to break through our lines. We were just as determined to stop them. Heavy mortar and artillery fire started to come in on positions along the line, but because of our isolation and the steep terrain in front of us, the attackers flanked around us and the rounds were directed to my right. A heavy barrage would roar in and then die down a bit before starting up again. It was terrifying to watch the battle, but there was also a fascination in what was happening.

Charlie Company on our right flank called for an air strike, and soon we heard the familiar sounds of the close-support aircraft as they came into view. Both F-80s and the slower F-51s were homing in on this one, so we expected a good show. In seconds they were over the target area, being directed by a small observation plane. The slow-moving spotter plane would weave back and forth in the battle zone, and when it had found the enemy, it would contact the fighters and give them the location. We called the spotter plane Cheezee, but for the love of me I cannot remember why.

The larger planes reminded me of vultures waiting as they circled for the kill, and then they began to peel off. One, two, three, eight of them flashed toward the ground to catch the North Koreans as they came into view. Then they dropped shiny, aluminum containers that tumbled erratically from the sky before us, as the pilots pulled out of the dives. Instinctively we cringed as these napalm containers hit the ground and exploded and burning gobs of jellied gasoline flushed the attackers out of the rocks before us. Someone named it the Devil's Brew. That was the most hideous and descriptive obscenity that could be given. Again and again the planes dived and destroyed, heaping clouds of black smoke and fire on the enemy. Then came the rockets and machine-gun fire raking, exploding, and finally neutralizing the attackers to our front. I wondered how any living creature could survive this holocaust. Still the airplanes continued their killing, coming around for another sweep. The men were ecstatic, shouting encouragement to the planes as the brown figures ran for cover. Even as I watched, feeling relieved that the attack had been stopped by the planes, I felt sympathy for the attackers. They were in the open, catching hell, and there was no place to hide. The combination of exploding rockets, machine-gun fire, and napalm had broken the enemy's spirit. I said nothing to the men as I watched the soldiers die.

Along our immediate front all activity had ceased. We were stunned by the concentration of firepower that had been brought to bear on the attacking force. It was the first time I had seen rockets being used, tearing indiscriminately into the ground around the soldiers below. It was as terrifying as anything we were to experience in the days ahead. Finally, after exhausting all armaments, the F-80s pulled up, slow-rolled in front of us, and left the smoking scene below. We were to see more air attacks in the following days, but none were more awesome or impressive than this first one on the Rock. With the attack broken, we slipped to the reverse side of the hill and made breakfast.

Within a few days we started to get some replacements, and the platoon grew from nine to twice that number, and then it tripled. The wheels were finally turning somewhere in this gigantic machine. The men arrived in no particular order; frequently several would appear with the supply train, or they would arrive one at a time. After the climb, they were exhausted, but as they straggled in, I met them and recorded their names when I had time. Most of them looked awfully young. They were scared, wide-eyed, apprehensive about going into their first combat position, but they were brave soldiers, too. Many of them expressed surprise that I was white – after all, they had been assigned to a black unit – but there was never a hint of animosity as they faced me that first time. (See appendix B for a list of platoon members.)

It seemed ages since the platoon had formed before me, and we started to get acquainted. In those first few weeks I had started to piece together a composite of the troops. It had been brief, but in combat one can quickly size up a man and determine, at least superficially, who could be depended upon when needed. Some were already gone, but the squad leaders were the same men who had come with the platoon from Japan or were present when I took over. Sergeants Mims, Hicks, McRoberts, and Rochelle were all that I could have hoped for. They handled their squads deftly and efficiently. At no time and in no situation, regardless of where we were, could squad leaders have been more dedicated than these men. Of the four, only Sergeant Mims was eventually killed. They were exceptional men and leaders, and I regret only that we lost contact with one another after the war.

Of the other men, the few I remember the best are the ones who fought well or who were wounded and left the platoon. In this group were the Johnson brothers, Gregory and Cordell. I remember Wakefield, "a good ole country boy," whom I'll mention later. They were all men who were brought together in an alien country to defend a cause they could hardly understand. They knew fear but generally were able to rise above it. They talked about home a lot, and several created songs about family and friends and relationships. Frequently, before we settled in for the night, I listened to the plaintive words as they sang of their loneliness and despair. I did not know the meaning of the word "blues," but I believed even at that moment that if one could have preserved the music, it would have been a hit back in the States.

Many years after the war, I now realize that I was closer to some of the men than others. That is not to say that I had favorites; the truth is that some men lived longer or stayed with the platoon longer, and I got to know them better. There were men who reported into the platoon only to be gone the next day or even before I recorded their names. But others stand out. Clark shouldered a BAR right from the start, never complaining that he had been dealt a heavier ammunition load. He was there when we needed extra firepower, and he used the weapon effectively. Robie Roberson was a slim young man who possessed a keen sense of humor, even when most of us failed to find the fun. He brought spirit to the platoon and was someone I reached out to because he was lighthearted and fun to listen to. Most of the men remain a blur in the memory bank today, but they were real people with the same dreams and expectations that we all shared.

I discovered this was also a time for self-analysis. I had been in Korea as long as any of the men, but I had not found the time to know myself or what was expected of me. In the first weeks I accepted orders without question; I was in a learning mode. I was learning something about the enemy, something about myself as a leader, something about the men in my small command. I had gained experience in battle and had grown up. I was confident of my leadership abilities, but at the same time, I wondered whether I should be doing more and how I should be doing it.

Combat for the infantry platoon leader is, after all, what he has been trained to do. To lead men into battle, to assume responsibility for his actions as well as the men he commands, can be frightening. A young officer has enormous responsibilities. He has to take a group of men and know how to motivate them, how to encourage them, how to correct or cajole or reprimand them when they do stupid things. And he has to do this with individuals who are different, who come from diverse socioeconomic backgrounds and educational levels. He has to understand, or try to understand, where they are coming from, whether they understand why they are in the immediate situation, and what is expected of them. The infantry commander has to be a counselor, a priest, and a psychologist. He has to be able to deal with the killers, the shirkers, and the men who will carry their load. Psychologists and sociologists study the mind and the societal setting of people and the why and how of what makes them tick. The infantry platoon leader, even without this training, has to deal with men in an unfriendly environment; he has to exercise control over them when they are frightened and hurting and hungry and cold. He has to be able to discern their concerns, understand their fears of being wounded or killed, and be accessible at all times.

The men looked to me as their leader in combat, but I think I was more than that. They counted on me to know when and how they should fight, and even when to back off. They expected me to keep them alive, to bring them back from a patrol uninjured, and to be in charge in any situation, however foreign it may have been to me, and they deserved no less. It was not a heady time for a young officer; on the contrary, it was a period of fear and frustration that he could not fully measure up to the expectations of the men.

So as they came up the mountain and reported in, I welcomed them individually or in groups. I asked them about themselves, trying to get a sense of the person, to learn something about the man and how each felt about the war and his being there. I believed, and still do, that it is important to the individual soldier to know that someone cares about him. At the same time, I stressed our relationship and let them know that I was in command and would accept nothing less than full support and complete respect. To almost every man, although there were a few exceptions when I could not spare the time at that moment, I explained our defensive setup and what was expected of them. I reminded them that most attacks came early in the morning and of the need to be watchful, to get their sleep during the daylight hours, and to observe certain signals in the dark hours. I told them that when they moved into their foxholes after dark, they should not move, because anyone shuffling around was fair game for me, and I would not hesitate to shoot. They listened to me intently; it was their first day on the line, and they got a quick lesson of war.

Depending on the composition of the squads, they were then assigned to a squad leader, who took them under his wing. Their training was just beginning. The platoon fields of fire were described, flank positions identified, and the expected attack route delineated for them. My basic focus was to provide as much information to them as possible. Sergeant Nollie would then take them to the squad leader, who would continue their orientation.

Within the first few days after we settled in, the initial contingent of ROKs arrived on top of the mountain. They were referred to as KATUSAs, or Korean Augmentation Troops attached to the U.S. Army. Someone in the army had decided that assignment of ROKs with U.S. units would be a good thing. When integrated into the unit, they could be expected to perform reasonably well, and in fact, after they had gotten into our routine, they did a good job. They looked very young. They had received basic training, and that was about all. There were ten in the first group, and I placed them in three of the four squads in position on the MLR. One could speak some English, so I assigned him as platoon interpreter. Kim Pyong Sum was a university student. Wearing glasses, he at least looked studious, and I was to find him of great value to the platoon.

The life of the ROK troops was not easy; they had been thrust virtually overnight into a war that they found hard to understand and even more difficult to cope with. As they arrived, wearing what looked to be cut-down U.S. Army issue, they appeared to be undersized, and I wondered whether they really were old enough to go into battle. They were not ready for bloodletting, of that I was sure. Their steel helmets looked almost ludicrous; they seemed to smother their heads, and their eyes were barely visible as they looked out at me from under the brim. They were small boys playing at the game of war.

They stood in a loose semicircle before me, gazing innocently at this dirty white commander to whom they had reported. I was as foreign to them as they were to me. Sergeant Nollie was standing beside me as I spoke to them through Kim. My speech was short and to the point. Dusk was fast approaching, and I wanted to get them into position before dark.

"Glad to have you with us. For however long you will be with us, this is what I want from you. You will be assigned to each of the squads. The squad leaders will be your teachers. Learn from them, for they have already seen the enemy close up. We are here to help you fight for your country. I will tolerate no slacking off. You will be treated like anyone else in this platoon; we share and share alike. That's all for now. I'll check in on you later."

There was no time for more, and I was not certain whether Kim had interpreted completely what I said. I called for the squad leaders and generally told them they had inherited some ROKs and should place them on the line and see to their needs. There was no argument; every squad was happy to get some additional men. They took them under their wings and issued ammo and rations and then returned to their positions on the hill and got settled in.

For the time they were with us, the ROKs never betrayed my trust. They went on patrol, shared our meager rations, stood long, lonely hours at night, fought our battles, and were wounded and died with us, and they never complained. They were brothers in arms, and they didn't let us down.

Sergeant Nollie and I talked about them frequently. They had arrived as unknowns, still wet behind the ears, but we knew they would grow up fast.

Sergeant Nollie remarked that everyone of us was already old before our time, and right he was. Every last one of us who had gone into action as soon as we arrived and who had suffered the agony of withdrawing after we had gone north was already a veteran and older than when he had first arrived. Combat changes men in so many ways. It makes them too serious, and I was guilty of the same emotions. It is hard to be happy or to express joy or laugh about the situation one finds oneself in or even to find some vicarious thrill. War is too deadly, and we spend too much of our energy trying to survive. Not one of us has time to dream of more pleasant things; we are too caught up in learning how to cope with the reality of combat. When one has not experienced it before, war, with its all-encompassing totality, is hard to comprehend. It is totally foreign to anything we have experienced. Our senses rebel at the sight and sound of combat. Little in our collective past has provided us with an inkling of what to expect, how to face it, and how to rise above it.

I cannot imagine what it would be like to go through that experience again. War, with all its excitement and death and destruction and adventures and challenges never to be repeated, is not for older men. It is for the young in mind and body. Only they have the strength and the resilience and the reserve to face the challenges and, having met them, to do what has to be done.

But while we had been bloodied, there were still a lot of unanswered questions. How would the replacements handle themselves in the defensive position? Were there shirkers among the platoon who would not carry their share of the load? Who among them were strong leaders, and who were just followers? Which men could be counted on in a fight? Which ones were the losers? The single person at the time in whom I placed complete trust was Sergeant Nollie. He had been with the regiment in Gifu, Japan, and certainly knew some of the men who were still with us, but the replacements were an unknown quantity.

I remember one, Wakefield, who arrived one day complaining about his sore feet. I attributed it to the fact that he had just climbed the mountain, and when I suggested that they would stop hurting after they were toughened up, he was having no part of that.

"You don't understand, Lieutenant," he complained as he hobbled painfully in front of me. "I just have a problem with my feet . . . they hurt all the time."

I eventually grew tired of his litany of complaints. "Well, it's too damned bad about you; you're here now and there's not much I can do about it. Cut the damned boots up the side, or get rid of the laces. But you're going to soldier like the rest of us." Then with a look at Nollie I dismissed the man, and Nollie assigned him to one of the squads.

Day after day he continued his complaining. His feet always hurt, or so he said, but he was a good soldier who carried his load. The men kidded him about his feet unmercifully, and as long as I was with the platoon, he never gave up on his complaints. Only recently have I heard that he continued through Korea, and by the end of his tour he had been promoted to sergeant.

One day, during a lull, I overheard a group of my men talking about a black lieutenant who had ordered his platoon recklessly into some action. It had happened earlier, before we got into our present position. They were venting their anger as they remembered the incident, and one even professed that the lieutenant would be "one dead nigger" if the officer ever crossed his path.

It was clear that the men expected their leader to share the risks of the action, whatever they were. I knew the platoon leader and had little respect for him, and I shared their anger. I could never depend on him to give me support, and he had caused me grief on a previous occasion. I knew the man who was ready to kill the lieutenant, and I was not concerned for the lieutenant's future. If he ever showed his face again, I did not doubt that he would be killed. Oh, it would have been seen as an accident, but it would have been final and irrevocable. The men hated his guts; he had forfeited his right, in their judgment, to be a leader again or even to live, for that matter.

That the action had ever happened at all was because of his cowardice. The men knew he had made the wrong decision, he knew it, and they could not forgive him for leaving them to fend for themselves. They considered him to be nothing, and they had decided to be the judge, the jury, and the executioner if he showed up again. The incident stands out because it was the only racial slur that I heard voiced the entire time in Korea. The men were willing to go all out for their commander, whether he was black or white, and it was clear that this officer had lost their respect. Only years later did I learn the specifics of the action that had caused the resentment of the men.

There were extended lulls in the action, particularly through the hot days, but in the late afternoon or early morning hours there was usually an attack along the front. Sometimes we offered our firepower to the adjacent troops, and they reciprocated when the attack was against us. It was a kind of mutual admiration society. The first few days on the Rock we built up the defensive position. As soon as the supplies arrived, we laid wire and set trip flares, and even took our empty ration tins and hung them on the wire.

We placed a few pebbles in each can, which rattled when the wire was moved, a sure signal that someone or something was in the wire. The beginning period was the worst, as we fought frequently to hold the position. On our right, Battle Mountain changed hands on successive days; on our left, "Saebuk-san" received attacks regularly, but the troops managed to reject the enemy just as regularly. The days continued to be long and hot and dry, but generally they were quiet and beautiful. The nights brought back the fears and cold and the long wait for the dawn.

After the sun had risen and chased away the haze that lay around us, we stayed on the reverse side of the hill, below the crest, so that we would not draw fire from "Jo," the name we gave the North Koreans. We ate, talked, caught snatches of sleep, and tried not to dwell on our thirst. One day one of the men went down the hill to look for water, and when he returned he was carrying a chicken and some raw onions. While we waited for the chicken to be fried (he used his steel helmet as the frying pan), we added chopped onions to our C rations. That was a real treat. When the bird was finished, we shared it around the fire. It was the only fresh meat we would see for the next month. We constantly watched for animals, but we never saw anything to kill, not even a rabbit or a squirrel. Rice would have been a welcome addition, but no one thought to send any. We probably wouldn't have cooked it anyway, since our water supply was almost nonexistent.

While we had sufficient food, the water situation was nearly critical. We usually started to look for the supply train in midafternoon, and finally the ammo, food, and water would arrive. The climb to reach the summit of the Rock was tortuous, and it was a long way up.

That we got the basics at all was nothing short of miraculous. Having made the climb earlier, and then with nothing more than what I was wearing and with only a rifle, I was amazed that the Koreans could get up as easily as they did. They had been hired to make the climb to carry the necessities to the frontline units. Each was equipped with a homemade wooden frame in the shape of an A onto which they tied the cans of water, the boxes of rations, and the ammunition and other items that we needed. I wondered frequently, after watching them come into the platoon position and unload their burdens, how many of us could have managed the effort. (Later in the war, General Ridgway, the Eighth Army commander, requested the ROK National Guard to organize and equip a Civilian Transportation Corps to support our forces, but

Korean workers assist in building an earthen bridge at the town of Shun-shu, August 24, 1950. *U.S. Army photograph*

at this time, I believe that each major unit had rounded up the carriers.) They earned every cent of their wages.

The priority items were water, ammunition, barbed wire, flares, and antipersonnel mines. Each time they arrived, we pounced on the water cans. Everyone was thirsty, and we were constantly asking them to bring more water. It was a precious commodity, so much so that water, however warm it was when it got to us, became the focus of our needs. The men would gather around waiting for the ration of water to be distributed, and they would talk about water, ice, a bath, and cold beer.

The litany of thirsty men was something I came to expect during the time on the mountain. They did not complain about the rations or their dirty clothing or even the lack of a field jacket to keep warm at night, but they craved water above everything. When the single line of Korean bearers got to our position and had dropped the packs, the water ration was the first to be distributed. It was usually less than a single canteen each, but infrequently the men got a bit more. It became such an overwhelming concern of mine that I sent a couple of men down the hill one day to see if they could find any. Partway down, they found a small spring trickling out of some rocks that yielded about three canteens worth of water in an hour. Whenever there was a lull in the action, one or two men would lug a can down the slope and patiently wait for the water to fill it up. They did not have to go to the bottom of the hill, but it was still a terrible assignment. The climb back to the top carrying a partially filled, five-gallon can could not have been easy.

Once I recall that "Jack and Jill" (as the men who went to the spring were frequently called) came up the hill with a bit more water than normal. The spring had flowed heavier, and they practically had to lift the can hand-over-hand to get it to the top. I decided it was time to wash with the precious stuff, so I half-filled my helmet and quickly washed some of the grime away. I had first washing rights. At least half of the platoon used the same water to rinse with until there was none left. It was a great moment.

As dusk descended, the men started to move from the reverse slope of the hill to their positions after having taken care of their personal needs. As they left, each man checked his ammunition or picked up a bit more, and then the squads looked over the flare lines and the barbed wire stretched around the perimeter. Our homemade alarm bells made from ration tins hung on the wire in the most likely areas of an approach to the position. Most of the foxholes held two men. This arrangement allowed one man to be alert and awake while the other man slept. Once the men got into position for the night, no one was permitted to leave his foxhole and wander around the area. I threatened them in no uncertain terms, reiterated my stance that anything moving after dark was fair game, and reminded them that I would not tolerate anyone leaving the mountain. They knew I was serious, and not a man was willing to chance my threat.

If I listened carefully, I could sometimes hear soft voices floating through the night, but for the most part, the men kept quiet, not wanting to give away their positions. Toward morning the wind would rise from the valley below, and the tall grass and bushes to our front caused our imaginations to conjure up Jo in every bush that moved. Occasionally a man would doze off, only to be abruptly awakened to some shadow moving, and he would throw a grenade, blasting the bushes and our sleep-dulled minds at the same instant. Men fired at anything that moved, and in the twilight of semiconsciousness it was easy to imagine the enemy moving in to attack. The firing was reassurance that the men were alert during the dark hours.

One night as I stood guard, I became aware of a swishing sound behind me. One or more persons were laboriously climbing the hill and were not taking much care to be quiet as they moved through the bush. It was about one in the morning, and the only light was from the stars. I listened and watched, straining to see in the dim light, and soon two white-clad figures came into view. I leaned over, touched Sergeant Nollie (who awoke and was on his feet immediately), motioned in the direction of the pair, and commenced firing. They dropped in place and disappeared. Nollie asked if I had hit them. I didn't know; they were hard to see, so I didn't have any idea. I suggested that we check them out at first light.

The shooting had alerted the men, who immediately set off some flares. How we loved having those flares! They made all the difference during the night. They provided us with insurance whenever we used them to gain sole advantage over the attackers. In this case, though, they didn't reveal anything. At daybreak we searched the area but found no traces of blood or any indication that I had wounded the intruders. The reverse slope of the hill dropped precipitously after ten or fifteen yards from the crest, and I had probably fired over their heads. I did not send anyone down the slope to check any further.

Infiltration was a regular occurrence on the perimeter, and units were faced frequently with North Korean soldiers changing into civilian clothes and making their way through the gaps in the defensive line. Behind us, in the villages, reserve units had captured some of these men, who were setting up ammunition dumps for the impending breakthrough. Just what the intent of these two were, I don't know. Perhaps they were to probe for weak spots in the line or to act as guerrillas in the rear area. At least we learned that we needed to keep watch on both sides of the line.

It became quiet again. We were left alone with our thoughts as they bounced across thousands of miles to homes and families and the girls left behind and even the more mundane functions of eating and drinking. During the night a flare would suddenly arc into the sky, and we would search the hills in front and watch the flare swinging lazily as it descended on its tiny parachute to the ground. Often small animals would set them off, but whenever they erupted, the men would watch carefully until they burned out. Then we retreated into our shells and our thoughts, one of each pair of us sleeping and dreaming, and the other watching and listening.

The first light of dawn was my favorite time. The gray streaks in the sky started to illuminate the land, and as the gray changed to a soft light, it reflected off patches of water that lay at a great distance. First they were the color of pewter before changing to silver as the sun came over the horizon, and then as it rose higher in the sky, they became gold, and another day was on us. There was an incomparable beauty to the place, this Land of the Morning Calm, but we were grateful to see the dawn. We had survived another night.

We were in pretty good shape. Other units up and down the line were not as fortunate, and the angry chattering of machine guns broke the still morning. Then the mortars started to explode, the thump, thump of the rounds forming the backdrop to the fighting. As soon as we felt safe from early morning attack, the men moved out of their positions and went to the reverse slope of the hill. Some built small fires to heat the cans. Others ate their rations cold, hardly tasting them, as the assault on other units was beaten off.

Sergeant Nollie and I made the rounds, as we normally did after breakfast, to check the ammunition supplies and the other items. I delivered a negative action report for the night, requested some things for the day, and then removed myself from the men to try and get some more sleep. The men, starting to get restless in one place, commenced griping.

Three meals were contained in each C-ration box, but it was always a treat to open the package and find something different. I believe there were twenty different menus, with assorted crackers and jam and coffee and dessert in each pack, so constant trading took place at mealtime in order to get something that one had not eaten the day before. Eating and making coffee were about the only things we had to occupy our time when we weren't fighting, and in our sector, things had been quiet for a few days. Heating the tins of food was an interesting exercise. With judicious handling one could strip the cardboard container into small pieces and build a small fire. It required a bit of patience as the flames caught and more paper was added. If one was careful, one could heat water in the canteen cup for coffee and still have enough heat to warm the rations. It took time, but we had a lot of it. Looking back now, I am surprised that we didn't get bored more than we did. I wrote nearly every day on the backs of envelopes and letters when there was time, and reread again and again the few letters I had received and looked forward to the arrival of the carriers who climbed the mountain. Of everything I could have hoped for, my single and continuing wish was for water – running water from a faucet – under which we could wash our bodies and our clothes. We all wanted that more than anything. The men seldom complained, except about the water ration.

There were a few laughs, particularly when Wakefield continued to complain about his feet hurting. The men joked about him and his problem more than any other single thing. One day I remember sending him down to the spring with another soldier. He didn't like the idea of climbing down or, for that matter, of climbing back up the steep slope. There was only a slight dribble from the spring, so the men were a long time in returning. Finally the two soldiers reappeared, holding the can between them. When they set it down at my feet and I made some comment about how long they had been gone, Wakefield immediately launched into how his feet hurt, and what was I going to do about them? That gave us our laughs for the day. Thinking about it now, I believe he liked the attention he was getting, so he played it for all it was worth.

One day after we had been on the Rock for at least two weeks, the Korean carriers brought us a large carton from the Red Cross along with our daily supplies. This was a red-letter day for us, I remember thinking; someone had not forgotten us. Now we could read some magazines and find out what was happening in the world, and my mouth fairly drooled for candy or cookies or maybe even a homemade cake. The Doughnut Dollies had come through at last. Before the carrier had a chance to drop it, we were reaching for it. Calling in the platoon to gather round, I slowly cut open the box to unveil its promises. It contained a treasure of utterly useless items. Bath towels, toothbrushes, and toilet paper flew from my hands as I aimed for the bottom. There was nothing else. A roar of laughter and yells split the air as the significance of this treasure trove hit us. Every item in the box begged for water, and we had precious little. We looked at the stuff strewn on the ground and could not fathom such a meaningless gift.

All I could do was shake my head. I knew that the box had been sent in good faith, but I could not accept the disappointment of the men. They deserved something better. The towels finally found some use; the men wrapped them around their necks to help stave off the chilling nights.

Then, for the first time on the Rock, it rained. A deluge. The men went crazy, using every container they could lay hands on to catch the water: empty ration tins, helmets, even the bath towels from the Red Cross to soak up the rain. They stood and danced and turned their faces to the sky, like in an ancient Indian rain dance, as the rain poured down, laughing and yelling like there was no tomorrow. It was great!

After the rain stopped, a mist hung over the mountain, and I began to feel a bit uneasy. The highest point on the mountain was shrouded in fog. Nollie and I talked quietly about it, certain that Jo would use the weather and approaching darkness to cover his movements. He was cunning and a master at using the weather to his advantage. The men, who were in the open, went to their positions and waited. Soon there was a cry and warning to look below, and we could see the enemy massing far in front of us. The fog got thicker as it grew darker. The platoon was waiting, tired eyes trying to see through the soup. Our imagination outstripped reality, and I prayed for the fog to lift. Miraculously, in a few minutes, it started to disappear. There was no attack on us that evening, but along the line at several places fighting erupted. Again, we had been spared a fight.

A few days later, on August 26, we were ordered to change positions with the left-flank platoon. They needed a breather. They had lost a number of men from repeated attacks, and we were to relieve them. When we arrived, the platoon leader and I went off by ourselves. I tried to get him to tell me something about the position. I wanted to know the likely enemy avenues of approach, where he had set up his automatic weapons, and his ideas of the North Koreans' intentions. I sensed immediately that he resented my asking questions. His one objective was to get the hell off the mountain. He was not very communicative. He mumbled a few directions and then, with a nod of his head, said it was all mine. Thanks a lot! Thanks a helluva lot! He called together what was left of his platoon and started down the trail that we had traveled. By nightfall we were in positions vacated by Able One. Early the next morning an automatic rifle opened fire, and looking to the front, I caught sight of the point men of an enemy force moving toward us less than a hundred yards away. The platoon opened fire along the line, and Jo scrambled over the rocks and disappeared. His maneuvering was shortlived, and there was no further probing the rest of the day.

I reported the skirmish to Able Six (the company commander of Company A), and after a brief delay he called back and ordered

Two men of the 24th ready to fire a 75-mm recoilless rifle at Haman, August 25, 1950. *U.S. Army photograph*

me to reconnoiter the area immediately to our front. I did not like the idea at all. First, there had been no need to patrol forward of our previous position; second, on the preceding three days patrols had received fire in the same area. The NKs had cleverly placed machine guns in the high grass and the rocks and waited for the patrols to come to them. It was the first time I had mentally questioned an order from the commander. It seemed apparent that sending another patrol was a useless exercise, but then junior officers frequently believe they know more about their own little sector than someone at another level of command. Since I had been on the mountain for several weeks at this juncture, I felt confident that it should be my decision to patrol and not someone else's. Nevertheless, I followed orders. The telephone went out about that time, and when it was restored a little after 0800 hours, I requested artillery fire forward on the ground where we would be patrolling. I could not get any. Then I called for an air strike, but the planes were needed elsewhere. Sensing the futility of the patrol action, since we had seen the enemy before us, I called for volunteers. Seven men stepped forward. They knew what had happened earlier but agreed to go with me. I asked Sergeant Nollie to call the weapons platoon and request them to throw in some mortar fire on the target.

I asked for the machine guns to stand ready with supporting fire if I needed it and requested our 60-mm mortars to lay in a few rounds of smoke to screen our departure. After that we started the descent. I had also ordered the remainder of the platoon to provide a base of fire if we ran into anything, and the mortars were again to drop smoke rounds to cover our withdrawal.

We moved very cautiously. I was determined not to risk any men. We were a team making a patrol into enemy territory, and I suspect each person was wondering if this was the time he would "buy the farm," or whether it would happen to the next man in line.

As we approached the point where the earlier patrols had been caught by the interlacing machine-gun fire, I decided that we could observe the area if we could reach some rocks on a higher knoll. There was an immense boulder on the rise surrounded by lesser stones, so I changed directions to head for the high ground. Other patrols had skirted the rise because it was more difficult to climb. As we started to move up, all hell broke loose. It became obvious that we had been watched as we made our way forward, and when I changed the route, the enemy started firing. My orders were to make contact and withdraw, and I ordered the men to fall back. I took no casualties. When we got back, I reported in and gave a status report and took a rest. It was Sunday, and I was grateful for that.

The routine on the Rock continued. Some days we fought off a probing action at dawn, and on other days we relaxed and enjoyed the weather. We found time to complain, listen to rumors (although as isolated as we were from the world, I cannot imagine how we heard them), and wait out each day. And then we received the welcomed news: we were finally leaving the position. We were ordered to prepare to move at first light in the morning. Prepare what? We had the clothes on our backs, individual weapons, and precious little else. The men gathered in groups to sort out the news.

Nearly everyone had his own idea of what was happening, and the men, so hungry for anything to grasp, usually picked up on the thought and repeated it over and over until it began to circulate as the truth. We were getting nowhere. Nollie and I had only gotten the word to move. There was no explanation other than that a unit would replace us. We were as much in the dark as the men, and so we put it out of our minds temporarily and faded into our positions to wait for morning.

As our relief arrived, we knew the ordeal was not ended. The unit was from a sister company, the commander of which told me we were going into reserve. That was the good news; the bad news he gave me was that there was fighting in the rear areas, so not to get too settled. At least we would get some hot food and have a chance to bathe and change clothes. We might even get an opportunity to sleep the whole night through.

The Rock had been a friendly refuge for twenty days. The enemy had tried frequently to force us off our perch. They had fought fiercely and died, as some of our own had died. Now as we climbed down that rugged face of rock, I felt something akin to sadness in leaving that place. That great, massive limestone formation looking over us seemed like a symbol somehow. Through the days and nights of our tenuous existence it stood defiantly with us. The scorching sun and winds and storms that buffeted it and us were now consigned to memory. I think there were others like me who, looking back, silently paid it respect. It was immovable, remote, and awesome. I would never forget it.

6. The Fight Continues

It isn't over until it's over. As we moved into position behind the MLR, elements of the 1st Battalion were hit again. I did not know exactly where, but the news came fast. A ROK police battalion had been placed on the line to help fill the gaps, and both units came under fire. In the meantime, my platoon moved into a bivouac area. Here we would receive our first beer of the war (we were issued only one can per man), our first shower and clean clothing, and some hot food. The men lazed around, refreshed and happy to have a respite from the fighting.

We got a new lease on life and for two days were able to relax and write some letters and read those from home. We tried to forget what was happening around us, although I was certain we would be committed soon again. I was not far wrong.

Trouble appeared to be brewing. All along the perimeter, the North Koreans applied pressure, especially on our immediate front and in the Taegu and Pohang sectors to our right and north. Then the Koreans attacked in great numbers on the night of August 31. The fight on Bloody Mountain was again joined. If I recall correctly, Company C, which was on my right flank on the Rock, was occupying a position at a much lower elevation than my own. And since it was easier to mount an attack at that place, control of the mountain had changed a number of times. There had been breakthroughs by the Reds, which were counterattacked on a somewhat regular basis. North Korean forces had gotten behind the lines in large numbers, so many units found safety only by setting a perimeter defense around their position. The reports coming in reported large guerrilla forces operating in the rear areas, and the support troops were as susceptible to attack as were the frontline units. Several artillery and engineer units were attacked and overrun. But rumors were rampant, and it was difficult to discern what was myth and what was reality.

Nevertheless, there was no doubt expressed about the enemy's will to fight or the seemingly unlimited manpower that was thrown against us. The North Koreans attacked aggressively and overran positions of the 24th close to our area in the vicinity of Haman, still with the intention of cutting through our lines to Masan. From the time the UN forces relocated on the Pusan Perimeter, the NKs knew we were stretched to the limit. The attack was one of the most vicious to date, and the casualties ran high as the enemy swarmed through the lines.

Elements of the 27th Regiment, or all of it, were rushed down from the Taegu sector, where the regiment had been holding the ridges for several weeks. The 27th was a solid fighting regiment that was frequently used as a counterattacking force throughout the division zone. My platoon was attached to the 27th to help restore the lines of the three frontline regimental positions that had sustained the brunt of the North Korean army's attack. For the next several days the action was a blur. I know that new battles developed rapidly, both on the line and in the rear areas. Not one unit, wherever located, was immune from the enemy forces that were thrown into the battle by North Korea. They had an obsession to break through to Pusan, and there was little relief in the fighting.

One happening is clear. Shortly after one of the breakthroughs, and after the 27th had arrived, I was ordered to find and to attempt to relieve a battalion headquarters that had lost communications with its regiment during the night. A single tank was assigned to me, and as it rumbled up to our location, I chose about a squad of men to go on the patrol. I checked the map coordinates for the lost headquarters, briefed the tank crew, and we loaded up. Riding on one of the iron chariots is a great way to go into battle; the feeling of power rumbling beneath one is exhilarating. I was not enthusiastic about the assignment, but riding the tank alleviated many of my fears. The morning was cool and crisp. We had to assume that the enemy forces were still in the vicinity, so we moved very cautiously until we reached the site of the battalion headquarters.

The headquarters was utterly devastated, the charred remains of both men and equipment scattered around for all to see. It had been surrounded and cut off from any support that might have been deployed to save it, and there were many casualties, the most that I had seen to date. How many enemy soldiers or guerrillas it had required to take the camp, I could not estimate. Nor could I imagine the cries of the men and the officers as the force struck them. I did not see much indication of a fight. Most of the casualties had been killed in their sleeping bags, and if they had awakened at all, it was too late for them to unwrap themselves before they they died. The horror of that first sight was sobering beyond words.

Blood was everywhere, darkening the ground under the cots and slowly dripping from the bodies that lay above. The smell of death lingered in the air, and the combination of blood and half-digested food and fecal matter made me want to vomit. Even now it is difficult to erase the image of that moment. It was a vision of death and the depravity of humankind so overwhelming that the senses cried out for cleansing. It could not be real. Men do not inflict such destruction as this on other men. But I was wrong, for the outrage was before me, and shockingly visible. Heads lay shattered, no longer sending impulses to the now lifeless bodies. The arms of several were reaching out, making silent supplication in their final gesture. God, dear God, what had happened there that night? Why such waste?

We looked at this maddening scene quickly. There was no need to say anything to the men. At their first glance they were shocked and saddened, and I do not recall any comments being made. There was a chilling silence that froze all speech, and the comprehension of our own mortality descended on us like a black cloud. As I looked upon the grisly scene, I felt revulsion, far beyond anything I had ever experienced, for the war that brought these men here to die, so far from their families and home – to die for a cause that meant nothing to the men involved. And I felt revulsion for the situation that allowed men to set aside the danger of war and lulled them to seek shelter in their sleeping bags from which they would never awake. Not one word was uttered; the mute reminder before us of the need for vigilance robbed us of our voices. Those who saw the violence never again had to be told to stay alert.

Now it was time to leave the scene. The Graves Registration team would soon be along to identify and ship the bodies. We left feeling utterly helpless, but we had learned a bitter lesson about war.

About half a mile away I found the battalion commander, wandering along the edge of a field, emotionally and physically beaten by the enormity of the happening. As I tried to help him, I talked to him quietly, to heal the hurt that he must feel, but he still could not comprehend the magnitude of the massacre. I felt great compassion for him at that moment, and for the guilt he carried with him from the scene.

For the next two weeks the fighting continued. The front lines seesawed back and forth. One penetration would be contained, and then another would be made. Then a counterattack would close the hole again.

As I recall, it was not an easy time for the platoon as we fought beside the 27th to restore the front line to its original position. Shortly after, I was ordered to rejoin Able Company on the line. If I had been given my choice of platoon locations, none could have been worse. The area that we were to reoccupy was very undesirable. The main line generally extended from the crest of one hill down the slope through a saddle and up to another. My platoon was placed in the saddle, the most obvious route for an attacking force to follow.

The platoon occupied the low ground on the extreme left flank of A Company. On my left, I was tied into the right platoon of C Company. When we got to the old position, Nollie and I surveyed the setup. We did not like what we saw, as the position was almost indefensible. Barbed wire had been strung haphazardly, and in front of the wire was a line of trip flares. I could not imagine the wire being much of an obstacle to the enemy, and although the flares would provide light momentarily, the numbers were insufficient to last through the night if an attack occurred. On my right, another sister platoon was in position. The platoon leader was beyond shouting distance, however, because there was a major gap between our units. There were never enough troops on the line in those days to establish a unified defensive line, nor could we create any defense in depth. There was just not enough manpower. I had rarely felt more exposed or uncomfortable with any position.

Farther on, about five hundred yards ahead, or to my front, the enemy occupied a ridge running parallel to our line. Between their position and ours, a large number of dead, bloated bodies lay. It was clear to me that the previous defenders had used the barbed wire to stop or slow the attacking force and then were able to kill them as they got hung up on the wire. Some of the dead lay inside the barricade, and I had a sense of foreboding when I looked around at the exposed location of the platoon and recognized the determination of the enemy forces to break through the line. I did not dwell on the matter very long, but turned my attention to setting up a defensive position.

Immediately to our rear was a small village, from which we could hear automatic weapons firing. I assumed that Baker Company was wiping up remnants of the force that had broken through before we occupied the position. Remembering the line-crossers on the mountain, I had to prepare an all-around defense. The majority of the men were facing forward, however. About dusk we drew the first fire on our position.

The incoming rounds were adjusted over us, but I knew it was direct tank fire coming from the ridge directly opposite my position. I called the company, and the CO said he would get artillery fire on the ridge. I could not understand why Jo was laying on tank fire, unless he had run out of mortars, which he could have used to great effect. He was smart and had waited until dusk before moving the tanks into position without drawing an air strike. But I was at a loss to know why the gunners were aiming through my position. Could they see something that I could not? They must have had someone behind me calling the shots, because the rounds kept exploding in the town behind us.

Notwithstanding what the CO had promised, I do not remember our artillery men firing on the ridge. If they did, the enemy must have waited out the barrage and then started to fire again.

Earlier, when the breakthrough had occurred, the North Koreans had moved quantities of ammunition into the town, along with some soldiers who were posing as South Koreans. I learned later that the sporadic firing behind us was the result of infiltrators who preferred to die rather than be taken alive. The tanks were trying to hit and explode the cached ammo.

The firing continued. When I heard the report of the tank gun, I would count the seconds before impact. It was quick fire, and the tank was aiming through the saddle where we had dug in. It was a terrifying situation, since we were located at a very low angle below the tank, and I expected one of the rounds to hit a tree. Then there would be a horrible air burst as the round made contact.

The holes in the ground offered poor protection. We could hear the rounds passing directly overhead. First came the whoosh of the projectile as it squeezed through the air, and seconds later, it would find its target. I yelled for the men to stay down and for Nollie to call again for artillery. He was already reaching for the phone, but he nodded in my direction.

Nollie spoke into the phone, then began arguing into it. I grabbed it and yelled, "I need some support. The rounds are passing right over the position; I don't give a damn what it is, lay in some mortars."

A second tank had moved up and joined the first, and the tempo picked up. Directly to my right, rounds started to fall on line. Some white phosphorus was being mixed in. That surprised me, because I did not know the North Koreans had "Willy Peter." I suspected they were using our mortars, probably a 4.2-inch mortar that one of our units had lost before. But the firing stopped abruptly as darkness fell, and we climbed out of our holes. A bit later, I heard a grenade explode, and an automatic rifle fired a burst, but we did not get into a firefight that night.

It started to drizzle, a light rain that was a precursor of what lay ahead. The days slipped past, one after another, and we stayed in position waiting for a continuing thrust by the Reds to push through to Masan. But for the moment the attack had petered out. There were still remnants of North Koreans behind us, but they were being flushed out and destroyed. Along our immediate front there was little action except for the occasional patrol to try to determine what the other side was doing and to pinpoint the weaknesses. That the enemy remained entrenched on the opposite ridge was not debatable. As was customary, I ordered the platoon to move to the rear of the hill during the daylight hours and cautioned them to keep off the crest. I knew that the North Koreans knew our location, but by removing the men, I could deny them knowing the strength of our force. Let's face it, though – it was a pretty pathetic force.

I kept the ridge in front of us under observation, and from time to time we could see movement, but the enemy commander was as cautious as I was. In fact, he had placed a sniper in firing position, and periodically he would fire at us. I requested and received a rifle with telescope to play the same deadly game and placed a rifleman on the line to return fire when we were fired upon. Both the ridge line before us and our own position were lightly covered with trees and bushes, and these offered some protection from observation. But for at least one or two days the sniping continued.

One morning the platoon was visited by the regimental commander, and as he arrived, the sniper across from us fired and my own soldier fired back. As the commander approached me and I saluted, he asked what was happening. I told him about the sniper and our attempts to keep him pinned down.

The colonel moved forward toward the rifleman and indicated in a somewhat derogatory tone that he didn't believe what I had just told him. "I want to take a look, Lieutenant." Then he raised his army-issued binoculars to his eyes to look over the military crest of the hill. I stood behind him and perhaps a few feet to his right. He was in the clear. Whether the three-inch silver eagle on his helmet or the glare from the field glasses was reflected back to the sniper, I don't know. The sniper fired once, and the colonel fell back into my arms. He was hit in the shoulder, and we removed him off the hill as soon as I applied a field bandage to the wound. His fighting days were over. (Clay Blair, in his book *The Forgotten War*, writes that this incident occurred in F Company's sector. It absolutely did not.)

On September 8 the rains came. The monsoons blew in from the south and hit us with torrents of rain that soaked us immediately. Our pitiful attempts to keep dry were to no avail. Everything was a mushy mess – the foxholes retained the water, and while we tried to place brush in the bottom to keep us off the ground, the water continued to pour in. We built little dikes around the edge, but they gave us little purchase as we went in and out. A few, but certainly not all of the men, had blankets, which they used to shield the holes, but the weight of the rain crushed the makeshift shelters. Our hands and fingers shriveled and cracked with the pervasive wet; our boots and socks felt leaden as we tried to move about, but there was no way to escape the downpour. Worse of all were the times when nature called, and we were subjected to yet another indignity. When we opened our cold rations, the rain slopped into the tins, but we ate anyway, in order to get some heat into our bodies. With the rains came chilling winds, and there was little warmth from the wet clothing.

We shivered and shook and remained cold. It rained hard; there was no letup. Now, as we fought the enemy, we also fought the elements. The foxholes became stinking, shallow wells. The dusty roads were transformed into sticky yellow trails of mud. And still it rained, day and night.

Around and within the platoon location lay the decaying bodies of the fighting, and the stench rose up and assaulted our senses. The sickly, sweet smell of death became nearly unbearable, and we could almost taste (or at least imagined that we could taste) the bodies as they rotted around us. I requested lime, and when it was delivered we shoveled it onto the bodies, only to watch the rains slowly wash it away. In this living monstrous hell, surrounded by bloated bodies, we huddled together for warmth and comfort, waiting for the rain to stop.

Looking upon this desolate scene, with the drenched men and the newly made streams that infiltrated in and out of our position, I thought myself mad. I learned there is no room for thinking even of better things. My focus was on the immediate front and as far to the left and right as my peripheral vision allowed me to stray, but of home and loved ones there were few thoughts. One cannot grasp the depression and loneliness that permeates the soul in such a situation. Except for the men, who moved slowly from place to place, there was no sign of life anywhere. The animals had burrowed underground; the birds had given up flying; even the enemy across the line appeared to be inactive. Perhaps, they too were looking for shelter from the storm.

But had the enemy paused, only long enough to perceive where we were and whether we were prepared to fight? Were they ready to launch another attack against our position, taking full advantage of our distress? Would some or all of us be the next line of bodies to be covered with lime? While we waited, the storm got stronger. Tempers became short, and more arguments erupted throughout the platoon area. Over such petty, insignificant things! Someone's towel had been stolen; another's blanket had slipped into the muddy hole where he stood because his buddy had not secured his side. The ill-equipped soldiers found little comfort in the fact that at least we were not in a firefight. What could be any worse? Morale was nearly shot; I had never before seen such depression and disgust in the men. I tried to convince them that it would soon get better, but we were in a living hell, and my heart and mind was not those of an encourager, so I was not very convincing.

Regularly, one of the men would come to the CP, oblivious to being seen or shot by the enemy's observation post, and ask to see the medic. I had great sympathy for them. The cold weather and the endless rain had finally done what the attacking forces had not been able to accomplish – reduce our fighting strength. Nearly all the men had fevers and dysentery, and our bodies were crying out for help. We had been reduced to the level of animals, leaving our holes to find food or to relieve ourselves and then returning to crouch again in them in the cold and the wet until we were forced out again. Never had I seen such an abominable-looking group of soldiers. There was no pride, no interest beyond caring for their bodies, however inadequate, and no shame. We had become a subhuman species of wild animal; our single need was that of survival.

About this time I became a noncombat casualty. Many of us had severe dysentery, but this time my abdominal pains wouldn't stop. I finally turned the platoon over to Sergeant Nollie and caught a ride to the battalion aid station. It was still early in the morning, and the wounded were beginning to arrive from the fighting the night before. Many of the seriously wounded appeared to be in deep shock. If they were conscious at all, most had been given morphine to erase the pain, and so the place was relatively quiet. Morphine, a derivative of opium, induces sleep and is a speedy reliever of pain. I have received it on several occasions and can attest to its wonderful powers. There is nothing that I have experienced that so totally makes the body so at ease. It is as if one is floating on clouds. It is another story when the drug is absorbed and the effect wears off.

The aid station could only care for the less seriously wounded or try to administer to the critical cases until they could be evacuated to the regimental clearing station or to a mobile army surgical hospital (MASH) for further treatment. The bodies of some men had been torn by mortar and artillery bursts that had caught them. One man was consciously holding in some of his internal organs under a giant compress as he lay on a stretcher awaiting his turn. Another lay on his stomach with his shirt removed, and I could clearly see where the bullets from a burp gun had neatly stitched across his back and had broken the skin. The weapon was a cheaply made automatic rifle, and although the ammunition was 7.62 mm, the powder charge was so light that it was used primarily for close-in fighting. The soldier had been lucky that the bullets had lost most of their velocity before finding him.

The worst casualties were those who had received hideous burns from white phosphorus shells that had burst too close to friendly positions. The burns caused the skin to hang from their bodies, and even under sedation the men must have been in tremendous pain. White phosphorous continues to burn as long as it gets oxygen, and it is almost impossible to dislodge. Earlier, one of my men had received a small burn from it, and although I grabbed some mud and placed it on the wound to smother the fire, it continued to burn. But that was nothing compared to some of these burn victims.

A sergeant who had received a head wound was carried in. There was only a slight chance that he would live. In the previous two weeks he had been wounded slightly three times, but he had refused evacuation. This would be the third oak-leaf cluster to his Purple Heart (the medal for wounds received in action) and would mean at best a long period of surgery and convalescence. I prayed that he would make it through. There were other men who had been hit by small-arms fire, and the lesser wounded were being treated by the medical corpsmen. "Doc" Carlson and Lieutenant Conyea directed the work of the corpsmen at the same time they worked on the more seriously wounded. I watched the doctors make quick, but thorough examinations of the wounded as they were brought into the tent.

The medics worked without rest, doing their best to get the worst cases dispatched to the MASH, where major surgery would be performed. The corpsmen were hopping, setting up plasma or IVs to stabilize the wounded, and they worked as a tireless team. They gained my total respect for the way they showed humanity for these broken men.

In an adjacent tent, other wounded waited for evacuation to Pusan and the quiet hospitals of Japan. When they arrived at their next stop and if their condition warranted a lengthy hospital stay, they would be sent to Hawaii or back to the States. The use of the helicopter as an air-evac vehicle was a godsend. There were a lot of men who owed their lives to the pilots who flew these fragile-looking eggbeaters in and out of the battle zones. In the hills and mountains of Korea, it sometimes took forever to get medical treatment for the men. The choppers extracted many who probably would not have survived a jeep or truck trip to a medical facility. The fear of being wounded was always on our minds, especially when we were exposed in some inaccessible area, because we figured our chances of getting out were slim. I know that bringing a seriously wounded man off the mountain required several hours. I have to believe that the physical trauma was greatly reduced by the flying ambulances, who raced with the wounded to a safe area where they could receive care.

I felt rather embarrassed to seek help after seeing the wounded and the dead. But after things had quieted down and been cleared of the immediate casualties, Doc Carlson examined me. He thought my temperature of 103 degrees and the dysentery needed some attention, so he sent me by jeep to the regimental clearing station. From there it was only a short ride to the division clearing station in Masan, where the city hall had been taken over as a hospital. The hall was filled with litters lying in rows on the floor. Behind the building, two enormous hospital tents had been erected to care for the lesser wounded and the sick and lame. They were filled too. I was examined again, given some medicine to reduce the fever and to stop the dysentery, and then allowed to sleep. I believe I was there for two days, in some euphoric state of limbo, during which time the fever subsided and the dysentery ended. Then I returned to the platoon.

The men welcomed me back with enthusiasm. We had been

together for several months, and they had become my family. In the few days that I was gone, the supply operation had finally caught up with us, and the men were wearing clean clothing and had received some hot meals. Just getting a break from the C rations had been good for their morale, and the single beer that was issued to each was a real treat. It was good to be back and to sense that my men were happy to see me. It made me feel good.

On September 10 we were greeted at dawn by a brilliant sunrise. The weather was therapeutic; the depression was lifted, and the men started to laugh and horse around again. We laid out our wet clothing and other items to dry and soon were almost back to normal. We remained where we were, anticipating probing actions along the front now that the weather had cleared. And then we received orders to get ready to counterattack in strength to dislodge the North Koreans from the Naktong River valley.

7. Perimeter Breakout

On September 15, under the direction of General MacArthur, the United Nations offensive commenced with the attack on the island of Wolmi and the invasion of Inchon by elements of the 1st Marine Division. The amphibious landing on the west coast of Korea, near the capital city of Seoul, was to change the direction and thrust of the war totally. While we were not aware of the specifics, there was a sense of lessening contact by the North Koreans, there was diminished probing, and the attacks had stopped. It was not until several days later that we learned the entire marine division was ashore, as well as the army's 7th Infantry Division, and was attacking toward Seoul.

Some of the North Korean units had already been pulled off the line on the Pusan Perimeter and had joined their brethren to fight for Seoul. That news in itself was cause for the Eighth Army to commence preparations to break out. At 0300 hours on September 19, something startled me from my sleep. The telephone in the CP was jangling softly. It was orders from the company commander to pass the line of departure (LD) at 0600 hours and to take the ridge to our front.

Dawn would arrive in three hours, and I was puzzled at such short notice, since we had been waiting for days to begin the offensive. Nollie had heard my side of the conversation and had already guessed what the message was before I rogered out. He left me as soon as he confirmed it and immediately went to find the squad leaders to give them the news. There was little rest during the next three hours; we were too keyed up at the prospect of heading out. I made the rounds to talk with the men, leaning over the foxholes to give them a short version of what had been ordered. Sergeant Nollie issued rations and ammunition, told the squad leaders to get ready to roll, and generally prepared the men for the attack that would start soon enough.

"Command" and "control" are two words in the lexicon of commanders that are used frequently to describe what leaders at every level are expected to do. As I went through infantry training, the words were indelibly imprinted on my mind. But the fact of the matter is that, although it is relatively simple to command men to do something, the control of them is the much more difficult part.

I could say, "Men, you will attack at 0600 hours, kill the enemy occupying the hill, and secure your objective." Or I could use simpler language and tell the men, "We're moving out at first light, and I want you to take that hill over there and then set up a defense." These are both commands that men understand. They are declarative statements of command. But I must command with total confidence and authority and calmness and act as if I am totally in charge. Finally, there can be no equivocation, no hesitation in my words. I must show that I mean what I am saying.

Command leadership is something many have attempted to describe. Talking about it in a military classroom is different from exercising leadership in a combat unit. As leaders, we are reminded that an order is an order – to attack, counterattack, or withdraw. But each of these orders implies that we must assess the situation on the ground, decide what the unit must do, and translate it for the troops.

One must have confidence in his men and his commanders. He must be able to make decisions promptly, adapt to the changing flow of battle, and execute without hesitation. Through his leadership he must let the men know that they can get the job done, that he believes in them, that he will look after them, and that he cares about each of them. He must instill, to the best of his ability, self-confidence in all. I cannot fathom command leadership, at whatever level, to be anything less. If my troops were to respect my leadership, I had to take the lead and not remain behind as they assaulted a position or as they stood and fought off the enemy but be with them all the way.

The control of men is different. The infantry commander needs to make a continuing practice of assessing his men. He must know whom he can depend on to lead and how they will perform, regardless of the command given. There are those who lead and those who follow, not willing to take any action unless they are controlled during the action. Unfortunately, there will be men killed before they kill, because they hesitate to shoot or do not shoot at all. To kill the enemy is, of necessity, what we are trained to do, but this can have some psychological effects on the one doing the killing. I have seen soldiers kill easily, not because they wanted to but because they knew they must. Sometimes it offers a catharsis for the soul; it is nothing more than a revenge killing for one of their buddies who has been killed. I have seen others, after a battle, become almost catatonic – men who are unreachable because of the guilt they feel after killing.

Control rests with the leader, and the men being commanded will have to place their complete trust and confidence in the commander. In all cases, he will direct the action, regulate the men taking part, and convince them that what they are doing is right. Control, in my opinion, in order to be effective, requires the leader to be among his men, encouraging and guiding them in every possible way.

In a fast-changing tactical situation, the leader must be prepared to cope with instant developments on the battlefield. He must redirect the action when required, and above all, he must be present – being seen and being heard. In truth, he must lead! After all, the infantry school's motto is "Follow me."

As a young officer, I was fortunate to enter the war with a new group of men. As we learned together, made mistakes, and had small victories, we grew into a small, cohesive unit. That is an important part of command and control. We became interdependent on one another, knowing that when a command was given, a positive response was expected. Control, while still necessary, became easier as we gained experience together and, perhaps in spite of ourselves, became of one single mind.

Now was the time to command and control in an attack situation instead of being mired in some defensive position. Able Six had told me that my platoon was to be the point platoon for the action and would be supported by elements of the company and battalion. The first objective was the ridge directly in front of my position. Having looked upon it for several weeks, most of the men had some idea of how to attack it, the direction of the attack, the hidden areas that might cause some problems for us, and how we should approach it. I had a quick meeting with Nollie and the squad leaders, and we made ready to cross the LD.

Our objective was the ridge from which the tanks had fired over our heads into the town behind, and now we were going to hit it for the first time. At daybreak we started the descent from our position and moved forward. There was only sporadic firing as the squad moved in a coordinated skirmish line. A few isolated pockets of resistance were found, but it was not until we reached the top of the ridge that we discovered the enemy had withdrawn during the night while we waited. When we got to the summit and secured the primary objective, we moved forward again. By the end of the first day we were located on high ground, where we stopped and dug in until the troops on our flanks could catch up with us. Here we had a chance to rest a bit, eat our rations, and prepare for a counterattack if it came during the night.

The next morning, as soon as we had breakfast, we were ordered to move again. This time our objective was a road junction in some little town that was considered to be a vital position for the movement of supplies and troops to the west. It was to be taken and held until the regiment passed through. We had just started down the slope off the hill when mortar shells started to drop around us. They appeared to be small rounds, probably 60 mm, and initially I was not too concerned about them. But as we continued to move toward the objective, the mortar fire became heavier. I knew how effective the North Koreans could be with mortars. They generally dropped a round in front of the position they were firing on, then one to the rear, and finally adjusted their fire to the center and laid down a barrage.

The line of attack could not have been worse. In order for us to reach the junction, we had to cross a wide strip of naked ground that led down and through the rice paddies. Then we could gain the ground to the left of the hill. Once we secured the hill, we would control the roadnet that centered on the town. It soon became clear that the North Koreans knew where we were headed and what the objective was, and they also knew the route that we were forced to take. There was no other approach available. From their location, which I could not then identify, they could easily observe us as we passed through the barrage they were laying down.

As we continued forward and reached the rice paddies, the volume of shells landing increased, and everywhere rounds were coming in on us. As the men started to cluster together, I commenced screaming for them to spread out and keep moving. For some inexplicable reason that defies logic, men under fire have a tendency to want to hang together, as if in the closeness they can gain protection from each other. Maybe it is the herd instinct, but I knew the clustering would draw trouble, and one unlucky round landing in their midst could devastate the bunch.

Sergeant Nollie and the squad leaders were yelling also. We all knew that we could not slow down the attack, and by moving forward it was more difficult for the enemy to pin us down. If we could reach the objective, we would at least be out from under the mortar barrage, even though we would be catching hell from small arms. First things first. We had to get across the paddies and onto solid ground. The squad leaders were pushing their men as hard as they could, but moving in the muddy fields was slow. Feet sank into the soft mud, and boots were transformed into giant suction cups that held legs in place. It was difficult enough without the shells coming in on us. Control of the men became paramount, and I continued to yell and threaten and encourage them as they moved across.

We still had not drawn small-arms fire from the hill, but I knew as soon as we hit the hard ground and could move quickly, the firing would start. Anything was better than being sitting ducks in the paddies and drawing the heavy fire. I was trying to check out the approach and figure how to attack the hill when suddenly three shells landed directly in front of me. They formed an irregular triangle. Although the leading squad was tactically dispersed, the explosions were near enough to knock out the entire group of eight or nine men. The only bright ray during the shelling was that when the shells hit the marshy ground, they penetrated slightly before exploding, and the mud and water absorbed some of the detonation. This time, however, there was no escape.

While the mortar was not entirely accurate, the rounds landing in close were brutal, and the men fell in place as if poleaxed. Several men tried to take cover in a riverbed but were caught in the firing. The medics could scarcely keep up with the men who had been hit. Those who were not wounded would frequently stop and help a man struggling to escape out of the paddies. How we managed to survive I don't know, but when we reached the top of the hill, the enemy had cut and run, and we collapsed on the ground, not bothering to dig in.

The enemy force was not quite ready to call it quits, however. While they had given up some sizable chunks of real estate (much as we had done early in the war), intelligence got word that we could expect major counterattacks at any time and to be prepared if they happened.

The platoon was tired. I had not seen them as physically exhausted as they were now. I made a point of relaying the information to the men but did not have the heart to tell them to start scratching out foxholes for the night. I believe I gave the men the option to dig, and some went to work while the others did not. I did not report this to the CP. Sometimes discretion is the better part of valor.

Although we had dispersed the enemy in our immediate area, the North Koreans started to move troops and equipment into the sector as soon as the sun fell, and sometime during the night they launched a heavy counterattack against sister units of the battalion. They were able again to penetrate, probably between friendly units on the line, and attacked the battalion headquarters, inflicting a number of casualties before they were driven off.

Fortunately for us, we did not get into a fight that night and were able to get some rest while someone else had the honors. As soon as the sun rose, I got the men rounded up, and we ate breakfast before leaving the hill. If I remember correctly, some other unit came in behind us in order to maintain control of the road junction the hill overlooked.

On the morning of September 22, near the town of Tundok, we continued the offense. The previous night the CO had given the marching orders, which were to attack the hill directly in front of the platoon location. It was a calm, pleasant day as we started from the LD, but it was soon to get too hot for comfort.

The men were physically spent. As we moved forward, another steep hill loomed over us, as forbidding as any chunk of real estate could be. When we got within the shadows of the woods that lay at its base, the men wanted to stop and take a breather, but I would not let them break, for the orders were explicit, and there was little sense in delaying the assault. I knew that the climb would be difficult. As it turned out, it was the worst mountain I encountered in Korea.

As we started the climb, the brush and smaller trees at the base changed into a forest of bamboo growing on the precipitous slopes. We had to climb literally hand-over-hand, from one step to another, as we squirmed between the closely spaced clumps. I had never seen bamboo this thick or so large. Frequently the men would shove a hand out to the man behind to assist him up the hill. It was a long, tiring ascent.

Suddenly I heard a whistle, and then grenades were landing among us. The men started to fire their weapons wildly into the trees and overhanging cliffs above us. We held onto the trees or bamboo with one hand and fired with the other. The explosions continued around us and in our midst, and the din of battle was deafening. We inched upward, and then a man would fall and try to regain the space he had lost. The grenades rained around us, but fortunately when they exploded, the force was directed downward. Those in the forward elements were less exposed to the barrage, and this encouraged the men to keep climbing upward.

For three hours we labored up the steep hill. When we got closer to the crest, I started throwing grenades above me in the direction of the automatic fire that was now pouring from the defenders. The fear of being caught in the fire ripped through my mind. It was becoming heavier by the minute, and it lent haste to my aching legs. Up to this point, my total attention was on getting the men to the top.

As I looked around to see the skirmish line laboriously inching forward, I screamed for the men to keep moving. Then I was out of breath; our bodies were strained to the limit. I had no energy left to shout more encouragement; they would have to make it on their own.

I threw another grenade, and suddenly the shooting stopped for a moment and I knew that we were about to scramble over the top. As soon as I crawled to my feet, I saw the first position, a large, artillery-blasted hole in the ground that the defenders had used for protection. It had failed, for in it the defenders, including an officer, lay groaning. The last grenade had done its deadly work and had shattered all three. The fragments of the grenade had ripped into them and had torn their bodies, and they lay dying. I immediately poured fire into the three of them and watched the life fade from their faces. The men were firing wildly at other North Koreans as they ran from their holes and down off the hill. A few stood and fought back, but Nollie and others continued to dispatch them one by one. The hill was taken, and it was time to look after our own wounded.

It was more than just an observation post from which the enemy had been adjusting their mortar fire; there were more soldiers than normally would have been placed in such a position. But the immediate effect was that the battle stopped the shelling of battalion units, so there was relief in that. After we secured the hill, I called the company and reported the action. Then I walked over to the hole where the three men died and removed the pistol and the holster from the officer. It was a Russian-made Tupolev 7.62-mm automatic. I have it today. We did not search the bodies. They were torn and bloody, and I did not need to know what they carried. The war had started to turn in our favor, and I had already received orders to move to attack still another hill that lay before us. For a few minutes or hours we rested and tried to cope with the weariness in our bodies, and then we started forward again, refreshed by the inning just won.

During that period of moving forward I remember several incidents that stand out as tragic happenings in the war. One day we had been ordered to take another objective, another steep mountain in our assigned area. To get into position for the assault we struggled along a track during the night. The dry season was upon us, but at dark the cool wind blew off the hills. Working up a sweat from the move, we got chilled each time we stopped for a short break, and the men opted for moving on.

The track led us into a small village compound. There were a few mud huts left standing and the remnants of animal fences, but there was no sign of any people in the place. We were always sensitive to groups of NKs foraging for food, so we entered the village slowly and by squads, one backing up the other. Finding no enemy soldiers, I called a break for the rest of the night, and after checking our location for the morning's assault, tried to catch some rest. Daylight was fast approaching, and we needed strength for the day ahead.

Again, it required herculean effort to push ourselves forward to reach the top. The enemy didn't give up easily, and the men had to be prodded forward to take the hill. There was some firing from the top, but I do not recall it as being very heavy. Nevertheless, as we moved forward, I requested artillery fire support during the ascent. I did not know what we would find on the crest, but landing artillery shells on an enemy is an effective way of keeping them in their holes to prevent them from firing at the attacking force. The artillery is trained to "walk up" a hill in front of the attackers for the same reason. I liked the classic employment of artillery that way; it gave me a feeling of security, and any time we could use the supporting fire, we did.

The men continued to fire as we approached the crest. Whether they saw enemy soldiers or just imagined them, I don't know. Perhaps it gave them security to help them make the climb. It was tough going (I can't remember having an easy climb, ever), but just as we reached the summit, we spotted North Korean soldiers running toward the ridge behind the hill we had just taken. At the moment we sighted them, and as I turned to issue instructions to Nollie, a friendly artillery round crashed into the hill directly ahead of me and exploded. I was slightly on the reverse slope, and the round came in over my head. I was instantly hurled off my feet by the concussion and instinctively rolled into a ball as I hit the ground. The shell fragments went whistling over my head, making noises like a scissors cutting a piece of paper. In the instant I regained my footing, a second round hit on my right. Again I was knocked off my feet, and I got up this time shaking my head as if to clear my senses. I yelled for the radio and called for Able Six to lift the fire.

Another round screamed in and exploded, and the men flattened out on the ground or disappeared into whatever depression they could find on the hill. Several were hit in those first few seconds. I screamed for a medic and then, to no one in particular, I yelled, "Now what the hell is going on?"

I turned and looked down the hill behind me, which had required such an effort to climb, and saw a dozen men already down the steep side about fifty yards, going hell-for-leather.

"Hey there, you bastards," I yelled, "Where do you think you're going? Get the hell back here or I'm shooting!"

When I first screamed, the men stopped shagging and turned around, waiting to hear what I wanted them to do. They looked at me as if they were seeing a ghost. They could not escape seeing the weapon I pointed at them.

Short rounds, as they are called, are demoralizing as hell. It is rational to expect enemy mortar or artillery fire, but never from one's support troops. Frequently mistakes are made in the heat of battle; it is a part of war. The men had reacted normally, I believe, and in their fright they had attempted to escape the shelling by scrambling off the hill.

The men sheepishly started to hike back to the top. When they got back, I reamed them out again and cussed their mothers and their friends and anyone else I could think of. It had not been an easy ascent. Like most of the mountains we faced, it had no identifiable easy way up. It was steep and covered with loose rocks, which made each step difficult. There was scrub brush that tore at our clothing and deep patches of grass to push our way through, and the heat on top of everything to contend with.

I told the platoon to dig in for the night and set up a defense. I was pretty upset about the whole situation, particularly for receiving friendly artillery fire when we had just reached the top. Besides, like everyone else, I was tired and hungry and scared.

I had been lucky. The trajectory of the rounds that had exploded near me had brought them forward just enough that at the angle of detonation the force of the explosion went up and away from me, and I received only the blast of compressed air. Others on the hill had not been as lucky. Sergeant Nollie and I started to take a head count. We found several wounded and dead. The wounded were dispatched back down the hill, and I removed the dogtags from those killed in action (the KIAs).

One of the men who had been with me for only one or two days, and whom I had not talked to when he arrived, looked like he was sleeping amid the craters. Unable to arouse him, I started to look over his body for signs of blood. When I could not find any, I assumed that he had been knocked unconscious from the concussion. Finally we rolled him over onto his back, and I peeled back his eyelid. There I saw a tiny hole where a fragment of the shell had pierced his eye and had entered his brain. It was the cause of his peaceful, permanent sleep, and I became angry all over again that our own artillery fire had killed and wounded my men. And I was also angry with myself for not being able to do anything about the incident except to report what had happened.

The dead have their own peace. Those whose lives are abruptly ended must have, in that instant before death robs the brain of all reason, the final thought of endless sleep. I wonder if in the final surge of mental activity the mind reacts this way. I know that however the death occurred to one of my men, I never found the man's eyes open, a grim death mask to challenge the senses of the living.

There is a difference between seeing someone killed whom one knows and someone killed who is a perfect stranger. The abrupt termination of a person's life is not a pretty sight under any set of circumstances, but when one has known someone, however short that time might have been, there is sadness in the thought that this life was too transient (especially if the person is young), that no longer will the person see a new day or enjoy what others take for granted. These were my thoughts as I looked down upon the dead, and I was angry that death had become the end of these young lives. Then my mind hastened to wipe it all away, rejected it even, and I became indifferent to the scene before me. Was it because I had gotten calloused with the death and dying that was ground combat, or was it because I recognized my own mortality and could do nothing about it?

I believe that we lose our sensitivity after a while. It is not that we harden our minds to the suffering or death of others, but rather that we have to move on. We may go through a period of grief or self-condemnation that we had not done something that could have prevented the death, or it may be a combination of both these thoughts. But whatever we feel, we must get back to the reality of the situation and continue on.

In our case, we went back to killing. The motivation was not revenge or retribution. It was simply what had to be done in order to survive. I am sure that psychologists had a field day, and they would identify what our true driving force was, but we did it simply because we had to, or death would claim us as its next victims. Killing the enemy did not affect us the same way as seeing our own men die. When one kills close-up, there is little sorrow or remorse; the most I felt was a brief thought that now the man would never see his home again, but as the thought washed across my mind, I rationalized that the killing was necessary, and there was not time to second-guess whether it was right or wrong. Yes, sometimes the stomach heaved for a second or two, and the bitter bile rushed from the depths, but then it was over and the other's death was of no further concern.

The war would continue, regardless of my thoughts. I left the dead where they lay and walked away. There had been enough killing for the day, and at that moment I did not care if every enemy soldier got away, even to fight again. Hemingway wrote something to the effect that "each time a man dies, we too die a little," and I had died enough that day.

Two or three days later my platoon was pulled aside, and the regimental units passed by us as we lay along a road, trying to catch our breath. I remember it was a beautiful day, and I can picture the remnants of the band sprawled there watching the men going forward. We had been the point platoon in the regiment for five days, and we were battered and exhausted in mind and body. I was again reduced to nine men; three of them had been slightly wounded and could have been evacuated for treatment, but they had remained with Sergeant Nollie and me. The troops had fought well, and we were now permitted to get some rest. That time, on that day, was probably the proudest moment of the war for me.

We did not know what progress the army and marine divisions were making in the Inchon-Seoul offensive, but we were very much aware that the landing and assault had been a masterpiece of planning. MacArthur had been right; its immediate effect was to cut the North Korean army's supply lines, which forced the retreat of the army from the southern extremities of Korea. The amphibious landing behind the lines had the secondary effect of relieving pressure along the perimeter, which was what the general had planned all along. As young and inexperienced as I was, I knew that the invasion in the north was the principal reason for our breakout from the tenuous line near Pusan.

It was also the reason why we had been attacking over the hills and mountains of Korea for the past five days. The distance we moved from the initial LD is unclear, but on September 24 an armored task force passed through the regimental positions and struck south and west to follow and attack the fleeing North Koreans.

About this time we received word that we would be transported by trucks and would follow the spearheading force. What a glorious relief! We no longer had to rely on "shank's mares" to fight up one hill and down another. So we loaded up and trailed behind Task Force Dolvin (at least for part of the way), which had led the charge from Masan on the perimeter and was on a roll toward Chinju. Earlier I had met Colonel Dolvin, and I remembered him as a tough tanker who had earned a high reputation in the division. He commanded the 89th Medium Tank Battalion, a unit that played a critical role throughout the first year. His units had provided support to us at various times.

The North Korean army was folding, but elements were putting up some scattered resistance throughout the regimental area. The task force was ordered to destroy these pockets of resistance and head for Kunsan, the division's primary objective on the west coast. The NKs did not want to be caught in a trap between our forces breaking out from the perimeter and those landed at Inchon, and they were delaying the UN advance as much as possible. It was "fish or cut bait" time, and the enemy for the most part abandoned its supplies and equipment and headed northwest. They managed to execute several serious delaying actions, but the impetus of the offensive rested with the UN forces, and we were moving quickly and making deep penetrations throughout the division's sector.

As we pushed after the rapidly disintegrating NK army and passed through numberless towns and cities, we were astounded at the destruction the air forces had brought to the enemy. While we had sat huddled on the perimeter, we had heard the claims made by the air force, but we found it hard to believe that the North Koreans were hurting for men or supplies to the extent that we were. Along the entire route, past Chinju, Hadong, Kurye, and Namwon, the burned-out hulks of trucks and tanks lay rusting in the autumn sun. In many towns the rail lines had been demolished, and engines and railroad cars that had kept the North Korean army supplied were scattered in the yards. Some towns had been utterly wiped out, factories had been repeatedly bombed and burned, and supply dumps had been destroyed. There were few places that had escaped the fury or the wrath of the air warriors. The firepower brought to bear was colossal, almost incomprehensible, and our eyes saw for the first time the destruction that had been wrought.

Korean civilians from Sangio line the roadside to welcome UN forces, September 27, 1950. *U.S. Army photograph*

Here was the proof and the results of the firepower, and our hats went off to the birdmen. We never doubted their claims again.

The offensive that had started on September 19 continued to roll. Now the shoe was on the other foot, and we found time to laugh a bit, and the men horsed around as we continued our ride. I vaguely remember stopping at night and bivouacking along the road, but I clearly recall one night being so exhausted that when we stopped, I found a flat pile of rocks, similar to the aggregate that is used to build roads, and without pause lay down and dropped off to sleep. It was a wonderful bed, even with its fist-sized stones.

During the day we stopped periodically while some unit spearheading the route cleaned out some obstacle, rebuilt a bridge, or cleared some area, and then we would load up and continue on our way. It became increasingly clear that the North Korean army was pretty disorganized, and enemy soldiers were left to fend for themselves and to head north as quickly as they could. A few units discarded their army-issued uniforms, donned the white dress of the civilian population, and commenced guerrilla operations behind the lines. While they were able to do some damage, they were not very effective in this role.

The success we experienced was contagious. I should give credit to the units that were leading the advance; our role was to follow, and this gave us more time to think about what lay in our future. We started to believe that we would be home for Christmas, or at least be shipped back to Japan and our home stations. The men accepted any rumor, however remote, and as it was passed from one to another, it grew out of all proportion.

By September 28 we reached the outskirts of Namwon. As we approached a bridge over a wide, shallow river, the convoy came to a halt. There were sounds of rifle and automatic-weapon fire directly ahead, and I assumed that the spearheading force had run up against some NK soldiers who were putting up a fight. Several vehicles had reached the west side of the bridge, but the truck I was riding stopped on the opposite end. The soldiers jumped off the trucks to wait out the forward action and to stretch their legs. About the same time the men were dismounting, a flock of ducks came into view, swimming serenely down the river.

Without waiting a second, the GIs converged on the river from opposite sides. Two groups of men poured down the slopes, like gladiators from another time, jumped straight into the water, and attacked the hapless ducks. There was no escape! The birds skittered to and fro, and the men splashed after them. Some dived into the midst of the flapping wings as the ducks scattered in every direction. It was now a race to see which truckload of men would be the winners of the contest. When the water cleared, not a duck had escaped. The men slowly came up to the trucks, holding their prizes high for everyone to see. One man brought a duck to the truck and handed it to me. I thanked him for it and tied it to the running board. Then we loaded up and started to move out, the men laughing uproariously as they rehashed the scene – the antics of the men frolicking in the water, and the sudden surrender of the ducks. It has been a wonderful way to wash themselves in the clear water of the river, a real treat, and the ducks would be a welcome addition to our diet.

Shortly afterward we rode through the town of Namwon, and by late afternoon we had married up with a new spearheading unit, Task Force Tolman, with orders to move directly to Kunsan and secure that city. There was again opposition on the way, and we settled down for the night to wait for resupply units to catch up. The following morning we loaded up and with other units of the 24th leading the hunt, got into Iri, a small town about thirty kilometers from Kunsan.

On September 30, after the mad dash across the peninsula, we moved into Kunsan. As the crow flies, the distance covered was about 250 kilometers, but we had traveled far more than that distance in less than a full week. From the time we were picked up in trucks until we stopped in Kunsan overlooking the Yellow Sea on Korea's west coast, the platoon had not been in any fighting. It was a welcome break, aside from the fact that we were tired of riding, and a great relief for all of us.

The natives were out in force to welcome us. Being cynical, I suspected that all the little ROK flags and banners had recently been removed from some hiding place to wave as we went through the city. I remember wondering what the flag of the People's Democratic Republic looked like, but I was never to see one while I remained there. I felt good, nevertheless, and after getting my orders for the night I found a house that overlooked the China Sea. It had a great view of the water, and I could have stayed there forever, or so I thought at the time.

While Sergeant Nollie got the troops squared away, I found the owner of the house, a wizened old lady, and asked her to kill and clean the duck. I asked her, again through sign language and a few Korean words, to steam the bird first. She understood, for she placed it in a large cast-iron pot after cleaning it and lighted a fire under the pot. Then she poured some water over the duck. Someone had given me a can of GI margarine, so when it was steamed, I indicated that she should fry it. At this point I could have eaten the whole duck.

I gave a few won notes to one of the men and asked him to find a large bottle of good saki (the rice wine of Japan and Korea). I was getting set for the evening. I salivated as the meat turned to a golden brown; I could hardly wait for the moment for it to be finished. When she finally brought it to me, I opened the saki and dived in. I nearly choked! It was the toughest piece of meat I had ever eaten. Then I remembered that I hadn't given the poor creature any water while we were on the road, and that must have dehydrated its juices. It was almost too hard to chew, and I finally gave up after trying for some period of time.

Whatever else happened, the evening was peaceful and delightful. I sat and watched the moon rise and reflect off the sea and drank my saki until finally I curled up on the hard boards of the porch and fell asleep. It was the first night in several months that I slept the whole night through without fear of waking to an attack.

8. Mop-up Operations

The division's objective had been taken. It had raced across the peninsula, spearheaded by two task forces: Dolvin and Tolman. The move had covered many miles, had smashed North Korean army troops, installations, and supply dumps, and had taken the city with minimal casualties.

Kunsan was considered to be one of the major seaports on the west coast and had in fact been considered as an alternative to the Inchon landing, but MacArthur believed that an assault there would have had neither the psychological nor the practical effect that it did at the northern port of Inchon, once the invasion occurred and the troops had moved into Seoul. Again, he was right. Nevertheless, the port had been used as an assembly area for the Reds and as a resupply point for the enemy force that had swept down the roads south before turning east to launch the attack on the perimeter.

Now we were ordered to take on several tasks. Bands of guerrillas and Red soldiers were still operating in the surrounding countryside, and we had been pressed into service to help clean up the area. We had hardly found time to get reorganized a bit, but the morale of the men was high, and the new orders seemed like a piece of cake. The enemy forces were for the most part stragglers who were trying to find their way north and were trying to live off the land, and we did not believe in their invincibility any more. In my judgment the men had changed into combat-hardened and combat-ready troops.

For the next few days we were sent out in the morning to search assigned areas surrounding the city. The native Koreans had been terrorized by the bands of North Koreans and were quite willing to show us where arms were cached after the enemy had fled. There were enemy ammunition dumps and other military equipment all over. My men found loads of small arms and a few fieldpieces, which, if I remember correctly, were still intact. None of the storage sites were booby-trapped (although I cannot to this day fathom why they were not), and we would load the material and deliver

Korean women and children search rubble for fuel in Seoul, November 1, 1950. *U.S. Army photograph*

it to some central depot for disposal. I do not know what happened to it after we turned it in. This period was an easy, brief interlude for all of us, and my house on the ocean was a fine refuge.

Our orders were rather specific. We were to capture enemy soldiers, if possible, and to fight any guerrillas that we happened upon. Although my men did not fight any actions that I recall, other units of the regiment did capture some, who I suppose were sent to prisoner of war (POW) camps that had already been established in the rear. The word "guerrilla" means "little war" in Spanish, but with the large numbers still remaining they were fighting more than just a little war. Their hit-and-run methods, especially when they came upon an isolated unit or a few soldiers, were truly disruptive. They could not afford to engage large forces or get pinned down in a long firefight, so mobility, albeit on foot, was their major advantage when they hit an unsuspecting unit.

On one of our search missions we came upon several young

men near a supply dump who were dressed in civilian clothing. They did not try to escape, but instead acted like the typical farm hands who were working in the fields. Since we did not see many young people, I suspected that they were deserters. One of the interesting methods of identification of friend versus foe early in the war was the fact that North Korean soldiers had entered the war with short-cropped hair, while the South Korean soldiers had longer and fuller manes. We used the test frequently to make on-the-spot judgments about the enemy. The few that we had captured early on had this distinguishing feature. Now, three months later, we could not rely on the method. I still was not sure about the men, and since we had no one to interrogate them, I dismissed the lot. We continued to load the materials and left the men behind after we had loaded the vehicles.

On October 3 we received alert orders for movement north. My notes reveal that the regiment moved at varying times, and in two days we had gotten as far as Chonan, a city about halfway between Taejon and Suwon. The 24th was to assist in securing the main supply route (MSR) and to hunt and kill any bypassed NK soldiers who had not made it further north. I was astounded to see so little damage to the town. The railway system and some factories had been bombed, and the rusting locomotives and equipment in the factories showed the effect of the aerial attacks, but the natives who had stayed behind, or who had returned more recently, were going about their daily lives as if the war had missed them. The black market was in full swing, however. There were piles of GI clothing, medicines, C rations, and other military gear, much of the type we could have used ourselves while on the perimeter. Everything was being sold openly in the marketplace, and I did not sense any hostility as we walked through the market and examined the abundance of "requisitioned" gear.

We must have bivouacked outside the town in a rural area, because my notes recall that the ancient way of life there was unspoiled by the war. It was a step back in history as "I watched teenaged girls, old before their time, pounding rice in a hollowed log, using hand-hewn stones for pestles. On their backs, their babies slept peacefully, as the rhythmic beating of rice lulled them to sleep." In one of the lighter moments of the war, we watched *The Jake Lamotta Story* on an outdoor screen that had been set up in a schoolyard. The elders led the children, followed by the rest of the people, who squatted to watch the pictures on the silver screen. I had the feeling that this was the first time they had seen a movie,

Young South Korean women carry water to soldiers near Seoul, September 25, 1950. *U.S. Army photograph*

and it was a reminder of how poor and backward the Korean people appeared to be.

We remained in Chonan for only a day or so, but I had little regret as we left and headed north to Osan. Finally, we entered Suwon from the south through the ancient gates that were opened before us. Suwon was the largest city I had seen since leaving Japan, and it was quite pretty. The route in showed little damage from the war. It had been retaken from the North Koreans on September 22, but I believe the NKs had already departed, and I do not remember any serious fighting having taken place there. Astride the gate, or perched above it, was a pagoda with tiles covering the layered roofs. ROK forces were scattered along the main street leading into the city, sitting or lounging in front of the buildings that lined the road. It looked a bit like a scene from a Western movie set, and the inhabitants of the town could have been the extras waiting for a shootout to occur.

What impressed me the most was the construction of the buildings. With the single exception of the division clearing station (back to Masan or Haman), which had taken over a brick building to use as the hospital, I had not seen solid construction of any sort since leaving Pusan. The few isolated farmhouses we saw and the villages we passed through appeared to have been built of mud. The actual framing consisted principally of cornstalks plastered over with mud to form the room or rooms in the dwelling. Suwon, though, was a real city with real buildings, some of which were two and three stories high. Many were surrounded by concrete fences, and there were paved streets and sidewalks. It was truly a different sight.

Able Company was assigned the role of acting as military governor of the city, which meant that we effectively controlled the activities of the civilian population. I had been promoted earlier and was now made company executive officer under Lt. Gordon Lippman. (Later, as a colonel, he was killed in Vietnam.) He was a fine officer, a strong leader, and we got along great right from the outset. I admired him tremendously, and the days I served under him were some of the best of my career. He was a hard, no-nonsense officer, but he was fair and an inspiration for all of us in that place.

I know that I gave Lippman a laugh once after we had settled down a little and he asked me to take a jeep to Seoul for some meeting, I believe. I remember the city as having wide streets or boulevards, tall office buildings, and very pretty residential areas that had come through the fighting unscathed. In the center of the city there was a lot of damage. I had gone to a hotel called the Bantu and was wandering around trying to find my way to the meeting when a fire broke out on the second or third floor. In helping to put out the fire, I fell through a floor when it collapsed and landed in water up to my knees on the floor below. The hotel had been damaged by the bombings or by artillery and was not in altogether perfect shape in the first place. I escaped with just a few bruises to my body but suffered some indignities when I returned to the street and my driver saw a wet and blackened figure emerge from the building. The soot and dirty water must have combined to paint a vivid picture of a sorry-looking lieutenant. When I returned to Suwon, Lippman took one look at me and collapsed in laughter. He did not let me forget the episode after I told him what had happened.

One of my first duties at Suwon was to visit and inspect the local jail. It was located close to the large school building we had taken over as our CP. It was my first time inside a jail. As soon as I arrived, I was met by the local warden, and I believe a Catholic priest accompanied us to act as interpreter. As we entered the first cellblock, I could not quite comprehend what I was seeing. The picture that overwhelmed my senses was something out of Kafka. The inmates were both men and women who had been accused of collaborating with the North Koreans.

Men and women had been placed in separate cells, which appeared to be about fifteen feet square, but each was jammed to capacity with wall-to-wall humanity. The scene was indescribable. The prisoners hung onto the bars, hands reaching through to beg me to do something for them, to give them food and water, or to release them, which I could not do. Animals in a zoo, I thought, as I passed between the cellblocks, except these animals had no room to pace or sit or rest. They all wore the white civilian dress, but they were pitiful creatures, stripped of their humanness and pride.

They begged and pleaded, to no avail. The warden had little sympathy for them. As they stretched their arms through the bars, he would strike them with the club he carried, and they would howl and cry at him, but he carried on as if they were the foulest vermin he had known. There was no compassion, no warmth in his presence, no forgiveness in his soul. He had a job to do, but I felt that he relished the control he had over them. They meant nothing to him; if he had his time in court, I believed he would have been the judge, the jury, and the executioner.

The place reeked of urine and worse, and I was glad when we finally finished the tour and returned to the compound outside. While I knew why the prisoners were there, I still had sympathy for their lot. I was never to visit the prison again; I had no desire.

The schoolhouse, and the compound it surrounded, was to be our home for nearly a month. The platoons were assigned rooms inside the building, in some order which I do not recall, and the men went about trying to find places to stow their gear. At least it was dry, and when it rained they were inside out of the weather. Several large tents were set up, one to serve as the mess tent and another to house the supplies that we started to receive almost before we got settled. Company headquarters occupied the space inside the front gate. Communications were installed to battalion (I do not know where it was located), and a functioning company headquarters group was installed to get back into operation. The

Captured women, who had accompanied Communist-led North Korean forces, October 18, 1950. *U.S. Army photograph*

initial requirement was to take stock of our equipment and ammunition needs, to replace what was missing, and then to get replacements to bring us up to fighting strength.

While I had assumed additional responsibilities as the company exec, I remained the platoon leader of the second platoon. This meant, among other things, scheduling the patrol actions that constituted part of our duties. Our primary job was to search out remnants of enemy soldiers who were still making their way north and to locate enemy supply dumps in the area. Since the route south led directly through the city, there were caches within the town and surrounding country. The patrols would leave early on their search-and-seize missions and then return in time to have chow in the evening. The time in Suwon seemed like peacetime garrison duty. We assembled the troops, inspected them, ordered them to clean and polish themselves and their equipment, conducted barracks inspections, requisitioned supplies, and generally had a brief respite from combat.

In many ways, it was a good period. The supply system started to turn, and we were pleasantly surprised to receive quantities of fresh meats and vegetables, which we devoured like madmen. The lettuce was something that I recall particularly, but we also consumed large quantities of milk and cheese and eggs, trying to put some fat on our slack bodies. The mess sergeant was a magician when it came to preparing dried eggs. Frequently we would find small pieces of shells in the eggs, which made us think that the scrambled eggs were fresh. It was not until later that I discovered that he would throw a couple of whole eggs he had raided somewhere into the pot with the powdered eggs and then beat them together. Why we did not become suspicious earlier, I don't know, since we never received anything but scrambled eggs for breakfast.

As brilliant as the mess sergeant was with the eggs, he outdid himself when it came to corned beef hash. Corned beef was packaged in gallon cans and in the processing was already cooked. Yet as the days went by and the hash continued to be supplied, he performed all kinds of tricks to make it a bit more palatable. He served it as hash, as meatloaf, as beef patties, as beef croquettes, even as meatballs, but he was never able to change the taste or the texture. It continued to be the army's same old quick food offering: corned beef hash. When we sat down to eat, we were never quite sure under what guise our old friend would reappear.

It was a good time for each of us. We played catch-up, and we enjoyed the regular hours for the first time in months. We read letters from home, wrote whenever we felt like it, read whatever we could lay hands on, and forgot about the war to the extent possible. I met a local doctor (another Kim) with whom I spent some pleasant times rehashing the war that had changed our lives forever. One night he invited me to have dinner in his home. It was quite fashionable, and I totally enjoyed the many dishes he served. They were a strange lot. I made it a game to guess what food was offered, but in the end the only thing I recognized was the ubiquitous rice and kimchi. There was a dish that looked like dried beef, but it wasn't. There was something that looked like fresh garden peas, but they were not. There was something that smelled like fish but tasted like tofu. Yet it was a fine evening, and I appreciated the break from my duties and wished for more.

Duty was a routine broken by a few memorable incidents. Several days in a row I discovered one of the platoon officers missing whenever I looked for him immediately after lunch. As the exec officer, it was my job to keep the outfit running smoothly, and his daily absence bothered me. I called one of the sergeants to report to me, as I wanted to get to the bottom of it.

I said, "Sergeant, every time I need Lieutenant H., he's never around. I don't know where he takes off to after chow every day, but I want you to track the bastard down. OK?" Check him in when we have chow call and see where he goes. I'm tired of that jackass taking off. Follow him if you have to!"

About an hour after we had eaten, the sergeant returned wearing a crooked smile on his face. He stammered a bit, not quite sure I was going to like his report. "Lieutenant . . . you ain't gonna believe this, but this dude has done gone and found hisself a house!"

"What do you mean, found a house?" I queried.

"He's shackin' up in town. Better come with me and see for yourself."

I grabbed my gear and followed the sergeant through the town. After walking about ten minutes, the sergeant turned to me and pointed at a house. "That's it, Lieutenant. Now can I get out of here?" I told him to go ahead, but to keep this incident to himself. Then I walked up to the door and knocked. It slowly opened, and I looked down on an old lady, a mama-san, who obviously owned the place, for she opened the door wide and bade me enter.

"Where is Lieutenant H.?" I demanded. She giggled and motioned for me to follow her inside. Pushing open an interior door, I looked in. The sight that greeted my eyes was mind-boggling. There, on the far side of the little room, lay Lieutenant H., lounging on a pile of pillows. He was wearing shorts, but nothing else. Surrounding his regal master were girls, about six of them, dressed as briefly as the lieutenant. Two stood near his head, fanning him with some kind of fans, while one lay on each side of him. The others stood around him as he lay there holding court.

For a moment I was so surprised by the scene in front of me, and the actors who were performing on stage, that I could say nothing. A memory of Arabian Nights whipped through my mind, and then my shock was replaced by anger, and I shouted, "Where the hell have you been? No one gave you permission to leave the compound! What is this, your harem?"

If I was surprised by the picture he made, Lieutenant H. was even more shocked by the fact that someone had discovered his secret retreat. He knew I was thoroughly disgusted with the place. His mouth opened to speak and kept opening and closing, like he was trying to catch his breath, but no words came out.

"You've got ten minutes to get back, or all hell will break loose . . . and that's a promise, Lieutenant," I declared for all to hear. He looked at me almost sheepishly and said, "OK, Sir."

I turned and left the room, knowing without a doubt that he would follow. I discovered later that after he had found the house, he had placed it off limits to the GIs during the day but allowed it to open at six in the evening. That way he had unrestricted use of the house during the day and no interruptions in the afternoon. It was almost a pity to ruin the war for him, but I had no regrets about the matter.

After the first couple of weeks, our supply of fresh meat ran out. We had gotten accustomed to eating again, and we looked for a change from the familiar corned beef. Our ingenious mess sergeant wasted little time in requisitioning from the locals. One day there was a great commotion in the compound. Looking out the window, I spotted the cook leading a skinny cow behind the mess tent. A moment later I heard a shot, and he came around the tent grinning like a clown. He had quickly dispatched the animal, and we all got fresh meat that day and the next. The bones were reduced to making soup for the troops on the following afternoon. There were few surprises better than this one.

The days faded, one after another. The routine that we had fallen into had become quite comfortable. There were many reports of scattered fighting by other units, but we did not get into any action. Not that we wanted any. We would not have volunteered any more than we would have requested a change of assignment.

The North Korean soldiers had proven themselves well. Now they were continuing to set up ambushes, find isolated groups of troops without protection, and then attack with whatever weapons they still carried. While some casualties were taken, U.S. forces constantly followed the enemy throughout the area and made them pay dearly for their adventures. Still, the North Koreans were able to infiltrate into our positions and attack at will, and the soldiers had to remain on the alert for any conceivable action that might occur. For all practical purposes, the UN forces had indeed won the war in South Korea. Enemy soldiers continued to assemble in the North, but many were captured or killed in going through American lines to rejoin their units. Our mission of holding the Suwon-Chonan-Inchon area was soon to be changed, but in the security of the school compound we gave little thought to future events.

9. Redeployment

On November 4 I wrote in my notes: "We awoke with the sound of rain beating against the broken windows. What a hellish day for a move! The poor weather did not generate much enthusiasm, but we crawled from our mountain bags, pulled on our dirty clothes and boots, and went over to the mess tent for breakfast. We gulped down a breakfast of scrambled eggs and bacon, bread, jam, and coffee. While we ate, Lieutenant Lippman went over the day's details. The compound, which normally was hard and dry, had become a quagmire of gluey, soft clay. It caked on the boots to form lead weights, a miserable mess."

Whatever the details laid out by Lieutenant Lippman entailed, the fact that it was such a lousy day for a move must have been paramount in my mind. Our orders were to move on the arrival of transportation, but the only vehicles available were three-quarter-ton trucks. We were still on the MSR, which meant that two platoons still on guard duty had to remain behind until transport could be arranged for them to follow. The rest of us packed our gear, rolled blankets and sleeping bags, and waited. While we hung around the compound, we wondered why we were being sent twenty miles to the south in order to load onto trains heading north. Several of us expressed our bewilderment when we learned that was the plan.

Who could understand the army's logic? I'm sure that the powers that be knew what they were doing, but it wasn't clear to me or anyone else. As we waited for the trucks, most of us still held onto the notion that a move south meant that we were returning to Japan. The rumor mill never ceased issuing bulletins, and I think they were accepted so readily because we wanted to go home. At noon, after we had eaten, the place grew quiet, each man absorbed in his own thoughts. What little laughter there was, was strained, and the men were getting nervous over the delay. The cold rain did nothing to lift our spirits. We were already depressed by the uncertainty of what lay ahead.

I continued writing: "The trucks finally arrived, and we loaded the men on board. There were not enough to take all of us, so with Lieutenant Tews leading the convoy, they set off. The trucks would return for the rest of the company. We policed the area to make certain that nothing was left behind. The main building, which I walked through to check if anything had been missed, was strangely quiet and cold without the noise and the activity of the men that I had become accustomed to. There was something sad about the emptiness of the rooms.

"I went outside as a truck carrying the first contingent of the 27th British Brigade arrived. I met a Captain Holmes, who greeted me very warmly, and then showed him around the compound. They had planned to billet about 450 men, including an anti-aircraft and heavy mortar company, and would be utilizing all the space. This was the advance party; the main body of troops were to arrive in a few days. They started to unload the rations from the trucks and wasted no time in setting up shop. In a few minutes they had a fire going and were brewing tea, making themselves right at home. I enjoyed tea with them, and it stopped raining by the time the trucks returned for us. On my way out of town, I stopped to say good-bye to Dr. Kim and we were on our way."

The 27th British Commonwealth Brigade, which had initially been deployed on the Pusan Perimeter, had been assigned to I Corps and had been fighting north of Seoul with the 1st Cavalry Division. It was now being shifted into a reserve position centered on Suwon. Holmes and I had talked awhile over our cup of tea. His unit had been moving since the breakout from the perimeter and, as I recall, had been in on the attack on Pyongyang, which was the headquarters of the North Korean army. By the time UN forces arrived there, it was lightly defended, as most of the enemy troops had headed north out of the city.

On November 5 I wrote: "We arrived at So-Jongni after dark, cold and dejected. It was another typically muddy, filthy village forced in between the surrounding hills. We were happy to bid it farewell this afternoon." It is obvious from my notes that we spent the night in bivouac and then most of the day waiting for transport to our next stop. Nothing happened worth mentioning, and we left in the afternoon.

On the sixth I noted: "At Pyongtaek, we bivouacked in a cemetery behind a bombed-out red brick schoolhouse, and while the night was cold and damp, everyone appeared to be in good spirits. At 0200, under a starlit sky, we ate and prepared to leave. It was still dark as we struggled under our duffle bags from the schoolyard over the narrow trail to the bombed-out station. Lieutenant Lippman gave me the rosters for those moving by rail, and after some further instructions, he left."

As the exec, I had nearly two hundred men to squeeze into three and one-half boxcars allocated to Able Company. Car commanders were assigned, and they promptly began loading. By this time, in the half-light of dawn, we distributed rations and water for two days. Then the car commanders began rechecking the rosters to make sure we did not leave a single soul behind.

"0645 hours. Car commanders again had a final roll call, and I issued instructions to each car." At this point I knew that we were going north. This was not a plan to send us into reserve or to Japan. I'm sure the men knew it too, and there was a solemn note about the situation as I instructed the key NCOs to orient their men in preparation for fighting as soon as we dismounted. I outlined how we would deploy and gave them the administrative directions that all would need when we got to the end of the line. I feel certain that I knew what the final destination was, but I cannot recall. Wherever it was, it would come soon enough.

"1000 hours. As could be expected, the train was three hours late starting, but eventually time won over the resisting Korean engineers, and we left Pyongtaek moving north." The loading and the waiting had not done much for our morale, but fortunately the day had warmed a bit, and we were not too uncomfortable. The bags had taken up one-half of one car, so we did not have a lot of space to move in. Interestingly, the men did not complain much.

"1220 hours. Ten miles in two hours and twenty minutes, and we finally reached Osan. Hordes of returning refugees stampeded for each square foot on the flatcars." There was another delay here as the train halted while the refugees climbed aboard. It was hard to refuse these people, who carried everything they owned on their backs. Although we had seen them before, they had never been allowed transportation. On our withdrawals they frequently crammed the roads with their carts and wagons, but they were generally forced off to the side as we passed by. We knew that some were returning to their homes or their farms, but some of them would find nothing left but the ruins. Almost all of them were dressed in the ubiquitous white clothing, and I do not recall any wearing a heavy outer garment to protect them from the cold. They did not beg for handouts, so I assumed they were carrying their food with them.

During our delay, we saw the odd-looking vehicles of the British brigade moving toward Suwon to the north. It was a large con-

A Catholic monastery in Tukone, near Wonsan, November 2, 1950. It had been burned by the retreating North Korean Army. *U.S. Army photograph*

voy, and I for one felt some resentment toward them. We had spent the best moments of the war in that city. We rested there, regained our strength, and had not been happy to vacate the place. Now, as we already knew, they had replaced us, and we were going back into battle while they stayed behind.

"We went through Suwon, and then Seoul after dark. We were now thirty miles from Osan, and by daybreak had reached Ilsan, north of Seoul near the 38th Parallel. Here we watched flights of F-80s and F-51s roaring overhead from the newly captured Kimpo Airport going north. Somewhere, someone was in trouble and needed close air support. Cargo planes, C-119s and C-54s, were also flying, obviously carrying in supplies and equipment for UN forces further north. It had been several weeks since we had seen air traffic like this."

At Ilsan, I witnessed something so unusual that I will never forget it. We had stopped but had not dismounted from the train for some reason. As we waited for orders to be passed, the Koreans started to get off the train. They generally waited beside the track, but a few started to go off on their own, perhaps to find a local village nearby or to make their way home.

Near our car a Korean woman squatted, as if to relieve herself, but almost immediately gave birth to a baby just a few yards from the track. She picked it up, looked it over for a few moments, and then dropped it as she walked away. We were so astounded that no one said anything. At that instant I thought how cheap life was, here in this God-forsaken strip of land running along a railroad. Perhaps the baby was stillborn, for I do not recall hearing a baby's cry, nor did I continue to stare at the small, pitiful body that lay there in the cold. Whether someone claimed the child I will never know, for the train slowly started up again and I lost sight of the scene, etched in my mind forever.

"Shortly after that we dismounted and loaded into trucks for our destination, Uibyongni. I think we all realized that we were close to being in combat again. The men were quiet, all the joking had disappeared, and the tension mounted as we rode over the winding trails. Just south of Kaesong we turned to the east and generally followed the 38th Parallel toward the mountains of central Korea. We crossed the icy Imjin River on a pontoon bridge and kept on moving. It was late afternoon when we reached Uibyongni, and I turned the company over to Lieutenant Lippman. After we had eaten, he assigned platoon sectors, and after talking quietly for about an hour, we crawled into our sleeping bags."

It had been a long, tiring trip. After we left Ilsan, it was just a short while before we off-loaded. I know that it was early in the morning when we left Ilsan, and it was cold waiting on the train. My best guess is that we traveled about thirty miles or so from the time we left the train until we arrived in Uibyongni. It had taken us the better part of the day, but I cannot remember whether we stopped along the trail or not. However far it was, I know that we were grateful to arrive and have the chance to get some long-delayed sleep.

I believe that originally the division was to move north to pursue the fleeing North Koreans by regiments. Perhaps they displaced as planned; however, around the first of November we started to get word of the Chinese involvement with the North Koreans. First we heard the Chinese were volunteers, but almost immediately we learned that elements of a Chinese division had been identified on the battlefield. As time went on, other Chinese units were confirmed to be in Korea, and together they would change the course of the war for months to come.

Notwithstanding this critical turn of events, Eighth Army on the left flank and in the central area and the U.S. X Corps on the right moved forward on the attack. The object was to secure the entire peninsula before the cold winter set in. There were rumors that we would be home for Christmas, that the North Korean army had vanished as an effective fighting force, and that UN forces were winning the battle for Korea. As it turned out, the first rumor had no validity at all, the second was generally true, and the third was partially true, at least up to a point. But with the entry of the Chinese the game rules changed, and we became pawns to be moved with great frequency by the commanders in Korea.

On November 9 I wrote: "Early in the morning Lieutenant Lippman and I made a reconnaissance to observe the platoon positions. The 38th was easily recognizable. The South Koreans had prepared positions facing north, while the North Koreans had dug in facing south along the line. Both sides had made use of concrete bunkers on the commanding ground, and elaborate trenches extended along the entire line of fortifications. How useless these defensive positions were! Looking north we saw the mountain ranges that formed barriers to attacking forces, but now the UN soldiers had simply bypassed them as they spearheaded the drive. The big question on everyone's mind was where the North Koreans were hiding, and how many would be found. It had been reported that perhaps an enemy division or two were massing in the central highlands. Our mission was to flush out and destroy them." When we returned from our tour of the company's sector, Lieutenant Lippman was called to battalion headquarters. When he returned, he gave us the word: Task Force Lippman, composed of Company A, with attachments from the intelligence and reconnaissance (I&R) platoon, one section each of heavy mortars, 81-mm mortars, machine guns, and 75-mm recoilless rifles, was to proceed to the town of Yonchon above the 38th Parallel and secure the town against any invaders attempting to seize it.

By that time we had gotten reports that with the entry of the Chinese in the war, the North Korean resistance had stiffened, and a series of counterattacks had been launched by the enemy against UN positions. We did not, however, believe that there were significant enemy forces in our immediate sector. The area into which we were moving lay a bit west of the central highlands and had been used as an escape route by units of the North Korean army as they crossed the parallel separating the two Koreas. That alone should have made it suspect.

The order now had been issued. Since we would be leaving in early morning, there were a myriad of details to work out. The platoons were ordered to clean their weapons and ensure they were in fighting shape. Each man was issued rations, and ammunition loads were checked and brought up to strength. Control procedures required considerable effort in terms of timing, supporting roles for the mortars and other weapons, and movement of troops. Company headquarters was to remain in its current location and act as our base of support. The duffle bags, which we had wearily carried when we boarded the train at Pyongtaek, would be left behind. We were moving with minimal personal gear and must not be loaded down with anything but that which was needed for the attack. It was anyone's guess how long we would be gone. I figured it might be for a few days, but not much longer, and was not very concerned about leaving the baggage behind.

It had now been six weeks since we had jumped off the perimeter, and I had already experienced enough fighting and the fear associated with it. The nervousness I felt on previous offensive moves kept me awake long after the preparations for the attack were finished and the men bedded down for the night. Dawn was only a few short hours away when I was finally able to shed my worries and fall asleep.

My notes from the briefing of November 9, while succinct, lay out the composition of Task Force Lippman and the order of march into the Choriwon area: "1st Platoon, 3d Platoon, ROK Platoon. 2d Platoon follows CMD. Cmd Gp follows 4th . . . 4.2, 81s. 0530 Interdiction. Displace on cmd, mtr to gen vic where 1st was, with fires north. . . . Displace 75s and MGs on Cmd . . . 0545 LD. Check radios. . . . ASAP notify Costello by msg when town is reasonably secure exclusive of mtr."

The Choriwon area would quickly become known as the Iron Triangle, and many battles would be fought for the high ground. But at the time of our entry it was just another piece of real estate that controlled the valley that lay before it. By this time the contingent of ROK soldiers had been made into a separate unit, and that KATUSA unit was assigned to the company to add strength. The order of march reveals several things: that the company was

Crew from D Company, 24th Infantry pose with 81-mm mortar, February 20, 1951. *U.S. Army photograph*

moving out as a unit; that we were displacing from our bivouac area by truck; that heavy weapons – 4.2-inch and 81-mm mortars, 75-mm recoilless rifles, and heavy machine guns (the last two weapons for direct fire support) – would be deployed as necessary; and that we would attack after interdiction fire had been placed on the town. What doesn't track in my memory is the vehicular move "to general vicinity of where 1st was." My guess is that it referred to the 1st Platoon, but that is pure conjecture.

Nevertheless, we crossed the LD at 0545 hours and started moving forward. It was a cool morning, but as the sun rose it became bright and warm. The main road ran straight through a broad valley surrounded on either side by mountain ranges. Since the valley was wide, we were not too concerned about enemy observation from the heights until we approached Yonchon. This was our first objective. It was just a few kilometers north of the 38th Parallel, the infamous line between North and South Korea, so we were passing into enemy territory at this juncture.

Our movement orders called for us to move into the area by leapfrogging one unit after another. This way, a base of fire could then support the lead unit. Normal procedure would allow our support weapons to zero in quickly on an enemy position if we got into a firefight. We moved by trucks for some distance through the valley leading north.

As we traveled along the road, we met a large group of men coming toward us. They passed us looking rather glum and did not respond to our greetings when we got within hailing distance. They were poorly dressed, and my immediate thought was that they were a labor battalion walking to some new location. I mentioned to the driver at the time that I wondered where they were going and made some off-hand comment to the effect they did not look to be very happy. We did not realize that they were guerrillas who, in a few short hours, were going to make it rough on us. Looking back on it, I find it incomprehensible that we did not stop and check them out, but the war was in such a state of flux at this point that nothing surprised us. We may also have been misled because we were in friendly territory and assumed that all North Korean soldiers had been cleared from the area. We thought we had nothing to worry about.

As we got closer to the town, we received some enemy mortar fire from the hills on the west side of town. Counterbattery fire was placed on the suspected location, and the mortar fire stopped as suddenly as it had started. We proceeded on into Yonchon, and for the remainder of the day scouting parties were sent out into the surrounding areas to look for signs of the enemy forces. Everything was negative. We wandered around the town looking for souvenirs and poked around the ruins. Little was left intact; I do not recall seeing one complete building in the entire town. The Koreans, with no place to live, had abandoned the place.

I found nothing of value; the pickings were less than slim. We ate our rations and relaxed. It had warmed a bit, and we were very comfortable while we waited for the patrols to report back. Sometime during the afternoon, while checking out another area of the village, I looked into a blasted building and discovered that part of it was still standing. On further inspection, I discovered that it was a bank vault, standing in the shadows of a crumbled wall. It was a finder's delight, and I decided to blast it open to see if it contained anything of value. I called one of the sergeants to lend a hand, and we found a gunner with a 75-mm "reckless rifle" who was willing to blast the door. I stationed him a short distance from the vault, and he placed a single round of HEAT on the locked door.

The rifle fired, the vault door exploded on impact, and the air was filled with pink banknotes settling all over the place. The men rushed to collect them, but we discovered they were North Korean won notes, totally useless to us. I have a one-thousand won note as my souvenir to this day, and a lot of memories of the terrible price we paid for our stopover in that town.

A few hours later, as the sun was sinking after a rather uneventful day, a truck convoy appeared in the town. My orders were to return to the company position before nightfall, but the trucks sent out could not transport all the troops, so some of us had to remain behind until the trucks could return. I loaded the first group, but as the last soldiers were struggling aboard, I had a premonition of danger and a chill ran up my spine. It was the only time in Korea that I sensed that something was not right. I cannot say today what it was, but it was as real as anything I have ever experienced.

As the motor sergeant turned to go, I touched his arm and said, "Sergeant, if we're not back within the hour, come looking for us." He stepped up on the running board of the truck and yelled over my shoulder to the trucks waiting behind. I repeated my request: "Get back here as soon as you can, OK?"

He leaned out the window and waved. The convoy moved slowly down the road and out of the town. As I stood watching the trucks leave, I could not shake off the uneasy feeling that I had. It remained with me until about an hour later, when the trucks came back and I loaded the remainder of the men for the return trip. There was still light in the sky, but it had gotten cold, and as the convoy moved from the town and through the rice paddies that spread out on each side of the road, I thought of the hot food waiting for us when we pulled into the company area. It had been a tiring day, but now we could get some sleep.

Then suddenly the sky fell in. A mortar or artillery round exploded directly in front of the lead vehicle, and as the driver tried to swerve around the explosion, the truck turned over and balanced precariously on the edge of the road. It was the signal for the attack. Whoosh . . . Whump . . . the rounds started to fall as the guerrilla force, which had taken us completely by surprise, commenced dropping a heavy volume of mortar fire on the convoy.

There were different explosions, weaker and stronger intensities of exploding rounds, but whether the attackers had artillery with them, I don't know.

There was no place to run, no place to hide. The lead vehicle had effectively blocked the head of the column, and almost as quickly the last vehicle was hit with a loud bang and was set on fire, closing off an escape route to the rear. Heavy machine guns took up the beat and laid down direct fire on the trucks, now filled with screaming men. They were pushing and shoving, trying to escape from the burning trucks and the murderous fire that poured into the trucks. Many were hit and killed before they could break free, and the trucks and men started to burn; then we heard the heart-rending screams of those who could not run from the flames.

Absolute confusion took over in those first few moments. An ambush, because of its total surprise, has as its focus the demoralization of men, and it is one of the most difficult combat situations in which to maintain command or control. It is the instant when men, even those who are combat-smart, react instinctively to survive. Some do react well, but for the majority the element of surprise shocks them beyond reason; their minds cannot or will not function normally, and it is hard to fight an unseen enemy.

Initially, it was difficult to determine the source of the firing so that I could set up a defensive position to beat the attack off. Men were yelling and milling around the area, some in shock, others trying to pull buddies from the burning vehicles to the safety of the road and the ditch beside it. The stench from the burning was overpowering. Still other men were dead, fallen like crumpled dolls, and some were dying silently around me. It was like a scene from hell, Dante's inferno, the flames and black smoke rising all around, the screaming wounded, the endless shelling, the swoosh and thump of the mortars.

Control was nearly impossible. I screamed too, trying to bring some sanity and control over the men, to bring order out of chaos. I realized very quickly that our only hope lay in getting to the reverse side of the roadway, which was raised about three feet above the dry rice paddies stretching for some distance on both sides of the road.

"Fall back! Fall back! Get behind the road. It's our only chance!"

The men were immune to my yelling, their minds numb from fear at the overwhelming suddenness of the ambush. Many did react almost instinctively, while others remained on the roadbed, wandering around as if in a daze, completely out of it, easy targets for the enemy gunners. The reverse side of the road was the only natural feature that offered some protection, which could be used for defending ourselves in place. Within minutes, those who were able had slid into position on the paddies, had reassembled, and had started to lay down a curtain of fire on the attackers.

I continued to scream to encourage the men to keep firing, to hold until dark. I had no thought that a relief force would materialize on the scene, nor did I know whether the enemy meant to rush us and join in battle. But I knew we were in a critical spot, and I believed that if we could hold off the enemy force until dark, perhaps we could still get away. It was the only possible option open, and I continued to urge the men to keep firing in the general direction of the attackers. By now the mortars had completely demolished our transport, and the shelling had been concentrated on the road.

Discovering where we had gone to ground, the NK mortarmen adjusted their fire, and we could see the rounds starting to move forward until they were dropping in the paddies all around us. It became increasingly difficult to see through the smoke and the darkness that was settling in. As dusk changed to darkness, white phosphorus and high-explosive rounds illuminated the grisly scene where we were stopped. The shells revealed the grotesque figures of the dead and dying. Some were beyond pain, while others cried in terror and pain. There were no medics to assist us that I remember, but the men tried to help each other to staunch the bleeding or lend a hand. It was a pitiful sight.

Finally, as it became dark enough that I thought we could slip away, I screamed as loud as I could: "Withdraw! Withdraw! Get the hell out of here." Then, as I watched the field ahead of us for movement, a barely discernable wave of the enemy started forward through the dim light to attack the flimsy position where we lay. Again, I gave the order to fall back from the road toward the open field behind us. There was scant protection in the field, but at some farther distance there was a stand of trees, and I thought that we could set up another position there until help arrived. At the moment, I had no sense of the number of dead and wounded who lay around me. The men started across the open field, and almost immediately the firing picked up and a deadly hail of rifle and machine-gun fire attempted to stop them. Some fell, stopped by stray bullets, and some continued on toward the trees.

Then the mortars adjusted again as the guerrillas tried to wipe out the rest of the task force. Several rounds dropped close-in, throwing me around as if I were weightless, stunning me for a moment, but then I was on my feet again, looking into the night. I started down the line of men until I came to Sergeant Nollie. He lay quietly, blood running down his face and from other places on his body, but he was conscious as I came up to him. I knelt beside him and reached out to help him. "Come on, Nollie, we've got to get out of here." He looked up at me, and recognition came to him.

"I can't move, Lieutenant, he said. "I'm finished."

I pleaded with him to come with me and offered to help him get up, but he refused. I argued, but it was to no avail. We finally said good-bye, and crying like a baby, I left him.

I looked around one last time. On the road where the burning trucks lay, ammunition started to explode as flames consumed the weapons left aboard. One glance in the dim light confirmed the dead who had fallen when they left the trucks. Beside the road, where we had tried to stand and fight, not a man was moving. The area was littered with bodies, broken and useless men who would never fight again. In my frustration and pain, I lashed out at the enemy, a lone figure who could not stop the advance. I laid my carbine on its side and fired until both clips were empty. Then I turned and ran like there was no tomorrow. Bullets cracked and whipped by my head, and as I ran, I remembered a grade-B movie I had seen. It wasn't real at all; this only happened to someone else, I thought.

When I got to the first rice paddy, I dropped behind the shallow mound of earth about a foot high that formed the paddy wall. Then I crawled to another point before leaping up to run again. I repeated this successively, not wanting to give the enemy a better chance to hit me. But then a stray bullet found me as I ran and gave me the impetus to zig and zag to escape the fire. I was alone and frightfully lonely, trying to extricate myself from a hellish situation that I could neither control nor understand. I was no longer a commander of a fighting force, and I could do nothing to change the picture. It was nearly beyond my comprehension, and I was afraid of death.

At last the battle was over. By the time I reached the tree line, the main enemy force had reached the road and was already starting to loot the bodies left behind. Single shots rang out randomly, but I was not to learn until much later the reason behind them. When I got to the trees, I found four men who had reached the sanctuary. All had been wounded except one, and he helped us in turn as we struggled on. Below the trees was a shallow stream, and we crossed it quickly on our flight for life.

We continued our race through the night, chased as an animal is chased. Continuing our move westward, guided by the stars, we finally found strength to pull ourselves up a steep hill where we felt safe from our pursuers. That night we climbed to the top of many ridges, came down the other sides, and bypassed sleeping villages where frantic, barking dogs hastened us on.

Much later, certainly after midnight, we came upon a large river. It was too wide and deep to wade across, so we searched downstream until we found a boat large enough to ferry us. We slipped it from its mooring, like thieves, and then paddled across to the opposite shore. When we landed, a steep, slippery bank lay before us. Helping one another, we eventually climbed from the river's edge and then dropped to the ground, heaving from the exertion. Despite the pain and utter exhaustion that permeated our bodies, we dragged ourselves along. Our strength was rapidly being depleted, and we did not bother to talk. Each man was quiet, alone with his thoughts and the pictures of defeat he had experienced hours before. I was still guiding the group by focusing on a bright star, and without benefit of a map I tried to keep going west.

As it started to get light, we came upon a cornfield. The corn had already been harvested, and the stalks had been arranged upright in shocks for drying. The field reminded me of a picture from home, but the vision was quickly obscured by the necessity of finding a hiding place for the coming day. I broke the men into two groups and told them that we would stay hidden during the day, and would move again when it grew dark. I cautioned them to check out the area if and when they had to leave the shocks and to stay inside as much as they could. Then we crawled into the largest ones to wait and sleep and pray for deliverance. We were cold and hungry, but warmth and food would have to wait, for I knew that we were somewhere in North Korea, surrounded by hostile troops.

Through the day we stayed in the cornfield, not venturing far from our hiding place, ever alert for anything suspicious. As the day wore on, we waited, sometimes crawling across the field to find water. We became hungrier and weaker, the cold seeping through our thin clothing. We did not have much hope, but we prayed together and alone, clinging to our faith. In the fading light, one of the group found a turniplike vegetable still in the ground.

It had been overlooked during the fall harvest, and we scraped the mud from it with grimy hands and shared it together, one bite per man.

As we finished our dinner, we looked up and saw two men approaching. Covering them with our weapons, I motioned to them to come closer. Through signs and a few Korean words I attempted to describe our condition and the fact that we needed food. They were armed, but one of them had a dirty South Korean flag tied to his rifle barrel, so I felt we could trust them. They were very young, perhaps sixteen years old, and they did not handle their weapons very professionally. The one who looked younger told us his name was Kim. That meant nothing, except that by revealing his name he meant it to convey friendship.

After we talked a while, he gave me the impression that he understood what we wanted, and then he got into a spirited discussion with his friend. After an exchange of views, none of which we understood, he indicated he would stay with us while his friend went for food. The evening wore on and there was no sign of his friend. I became suspicious; it should not have taken that amount of time to get some food. Finally I insisted that we had to move, and throwing my arm around Kim's small shoulders, I urged him forward. We crossed the field and started down a winding path leading toward a village. My left arm was over his shoulder which helped support my body, and I cradled my carbine in my right hand with the muzzle across my chest aimed at Kim. I was not certain where we were going or what lay ahead, but I had decided to shoot him if we were caught again. He smiled at me and continued to support me as we walked slowly down the path.

Suddenly Kim pulled up short and, without waiting to see what my reaction would be, fired a shot into the air. The light dawned on me. He had chambered a round before he came up to us and could have shot any one of us had he chosen to do so. I was instantly on guard. Almost immediately there was an answering shot from the village. I was reluctant to continue walking, but after another go at sign language, he convinced me that food was being prepared for us and we could eat as soon as we arrived. (It was not until later that I learned about Kim's prearranged signal. His friend had preceded us into the town to make sure the coast was clear. If there had been enemy soldiers in the village, no answering shot would have been fired.) It was safe to enter, and I was suddenly tired beyond belief as we slipped into the town.

All the elders of the village were on hand to greet us. They were retired farmers, who, I was to learn later, have a place of high honor in traditional Korean culture. Their symbol of authority is a high, black horsehair hat (although I never saw a horse anywhere during my tour) perched on the head and tied under the chin. It is also a sign of respect. The elders looked quite smashing, with their hats and their white trousers gathered at the ankle, then covered with a full-length, wide-sleeved coat reaching to the knees.

They had already selected a small house and led us to it. Some of them returned shortly bearing a pot of soup and a platter of dried beef. The highly seasoned kimchi was set before us. Greedily, we reached for the common bowl of pap (rice) and added the rice and beef to the steaming soup. The earthen bowls were large, and our stomachs were small from the enforced fasting, but we stuffed ourselves without pausing to talk. We were famished, and we made short work of the meal. Another delicacy was offered, the so-called hundred-year-old eggs, but we turned them down and, to be polite, gestured that our stomachs were full by patting and laughing and talking to each other. I don't think I could have managed the eggs. They had been buried for months ripening, and the yolks had turned black and the whites blue. We could not feast upon them. Our hosts did not insist.

As might be expected, as soon as we ate we became very sleepy. The warmth of the house (heated by a fire of small branches and twigs under the house in a firebox) and the food and the apparent safety lulled us into sleep quickly, and we stretched out on the floor, a tired and happy group of men who had made it this far.

About midnight, Kim woke us and indicated that he would take us to another village. On the way I learned that he had stood guard over us as we slept in case we had to move suddenly into the hills. I do not remember how far we walked, but finally he delivered us to a South Korean police station, which fortunately had a telephone tied into U.S. lines, and I was able to report directly to someone at battalion. They immediately arranged to have an ambulance meet us early in the morning. They did not feel it was safe to attempt a pickup during the night, because there had been several attacks made by guerrilla bands on small groups of men or vehicles traveling after dark without escorts.

Kim elected to stay with us, although I encouraged him to return to his village. We found someplace to sleep again in the station, but I was so excited about our escape and imminent rescue that I just lay down and rested. As we were being helped into the waiting ambulances, we thanked this lad who had brought us through the recent nightmare. The only possession I had that I thought he might use was a shiny aluminum pipe. When I gave it to him, attempting to tell him how we felt about him, my emotions overcame me, and I held him close for a few moments. It was a sad departure. I knew that I would probably never see Kim again, in a land of many Kims, but I would always be grateful to him for his friendship and a faith made stronger because of him. His name was Kim Pyong Sum of Marjon, a young lad who had compassion, courage, and love, and one I will long remember.

When I got to the hospital and woke up the first day, there in the cot beside me was Sergeant Nollie, whom I had left for dead beside the road! He told me what had happened. After I left, he crawled away, covered himself with the blood from his wounds, coated his face with blood, and pretended to be dead. The North Koreans discovered him, assumed he was dead, and removed his boots before leaving. In the morning he was found alive and was brought to the hospital and placed beside me in the ward.

Thirty-eight men died in the ambush. Only Nollie and I and a few others survived. The attacking force was estimated to have numbered six hundred North Korean irregular soldiers. From a hospital bed in Tokyo, on December 15, I wrote home about the action. My letter reads in part: "I'm sending a clipping which describes in some respects what happened. I was the Exec of the company, and at the time, had about 60 men with me, or attached. The I&R Platoon was attached, but was not covering the withdrawal as it states. Several men, in fact two whom I know, escaped after being taken prisoners, and at least four have not been found. I was hit attempting to set up a defense so we could wait until dark, but as usual the flanks were open and they [the enemy] came in."

The 25th Infantry Division reported in *Battleground Korea* a summary statement about the ambush and a description of the attack on the town of Yonchon. It is almost an understatement of the events of that day. It reads: "Company A of the 24th RCT launched a coordinated attack on the town of Yonchon with elements of the 17th ROK Regiment and 800 South Korean policemen. Striking in the early morning after a preliminary 30-minute mortar barrage, this UN force captured the town in less than three hours. Thirteen North Korean soldiers were captured. Later in the day the I&R Platoon with elements of Company A of the 24th were ambushed. The enemy knocked out the lead and rear vehicles of the convoy and set several afire. As members of the American patrol leapt from their vehicles to defend themselves, the Reds charged and inflicted heavy casualties."

It was not the first ambush that had hit division troops, and it would not be the last. The North Koreans continued to use this form of attack frequently in the days ahead, and UN forces would take heavy casualties as they continued.

10. Time Out

Sometime, one or several days after arriving at the hospital, we were placed on a hospital bus that carried us to Kimpo Airport near Seoul for evacuation to Japan. Air traffic was heavy that day as we waited in the buses, but our flight eventually arrived. The litters were placed on the plane, and we got airborne. Predictably, the plane was full. The litters were hung from racks attached to the fuselage, and there was very little space between them. They ran head to foot down the sides of the airplane, and the litter above me was scant inches from my face. No one was complaining; we were happy to be returning to Japan, however brief our stay would be. It was a wonderful feeling to be leaving Korea, and I for one hoped it would be for good. The men were expressing their thoughts aloud, and seeing the air force nurses filled us with joy. They were a treat for the eyes, and they treated each of us with loving care for the short trip back.

While the plane waited for clearance to leave, I thought about one of the women who had sailed with me from the States to Japan months earlier. She was going to meet her husband, Bob Porter, who was assigned to some unit near Tokyo. She had volunteered to work as the ship's librarian during the crossing, and we struck up an acquaintance when I visited the library. Alta was a lovely person whom I treated as a big sister. It was great to spend time together on the trip, and we had a lot of laughs and fun. She was willing to listen to whatever problem I had aboard the ship, and I appreciated her kindness and her understanding.

When we disembarked in Yokohama, she asked me to keep in touch, and the following Christmas I was able to meet Bob when I visited them in the Tokyo area. They helped me through a lonely holiday season, and I got to know Bob and it was a good time. We kept in touch periodically after I went off to Korea. Alta told me that she had become a Red Cross Grey Lady and was meeting the medical evacuation flights arriving from Korea. In my last letter to her I had written, "I won't be coming back through Itazuki [where she was working], but I hope to see you all soon." I did not expect to become a statistic, but events were not controllable, and here I was on my way to Japan and the base at Itazuki.

The medical buses were on the ramp as soon as we landed, and as I was being transfered from the airplane, I looked up, and there was Alta! We greeted each other as old friends, and she accompanied me to the hospital. While I was being processed in, we talked about past events and friends we knew and then said good-bye. I was not to see Bob and her again for several years. I remained in the base hospital briefly and then was transferred to the Tokyo Army Hospital for further determination of medical treatment that might be required.

Tokyo Army Hospital was the final decision-making authority for the wounded. It was there that an assessment of the patient's condition was made, and when that was completed, it was determined whether the patient remained in Japan for treatment or returned to the States. The prognosis in my case was that I would not require lengthy medical care and eventually would be returned to Korea. That was bad news.

I was assigned to a room that was shared by an officer who had received a bad chest wound. He had been shot through the lungs, so he was in a lot worse condition than I. My roommate was the son of a well-known, very senior army general, and he had a constant flow of visitors who had known his family. I believe he was married at the time, but whatever his situation, we had a room filled with flowers and gifts and a lot of traffic in and out. He was taciturn, but we got along well. I did not have that many friends in Japan, but those who learned of my hospital stay came to visit and brought gifts of food and comfort that I really appreciated.

During my time there I met several officers whom I had known in the States, and we reminisced about our time at Fort Benning. I found one of them in the snack bar sharing lunch with a young, pretty Department of the Army civilian (DAC) who was working in Tokyo. He too had been wounded and was on his way out of the hospital and returning to Korea. Like me, he wasn't very excited about the prospect.

As soon as I became ambulatory, I took advantage of the facilities within the hospital. It was wonderful to leave my room and see the grounds around the hospital and to visit the mess hall or the snack bar. I never tired of ordering hamburgers and French fries and tall milk shakes. I was in heaven, eating whatever was placed before me, drinking water from a fountain or the pitcher placed beside the bed, sleeping on clean sheets, and reading to my heart's content. Fortunately, I was aware at the time, and not just as an afterthought, how wonderful it was to be in Tokyo.

As the news of the fighting was reported, particularly in the central area of Korea, close to where I had been wounded, I felt grateful to be where I was. I remembered that before we had gotten orders to leave Suwon, the first reports had filtered down of North Korean troops who could speak only Chinese. By November 6, Chinese Communist soldiers had been positively identified and were on a roll. That was the same time that Able Company was on the way north by rail to Uibyongni. I also suspect that the company had not been told to expect Chinese forces. Whether Lieutenant Lippman knew it at the time is doubtful. He and I were close, and I am certain he would have told me if he had known and would have asked me to keep the news secret.

In retrospect, one of the great failures of the Korean War was the lack of information concerning Chinese intent. This was to remain a continuing problem and would affect the army commander's strategic planning ability in the weeks ahead. Intelligence at every level of command on enemy units, their size, and their disposition was difficult to obtain and analyze and sporadic at best. Intelligence units found it extremely hard to sort out fact from fiction, and the analyses generated provided little usable information upon which commanders could make decisions.

It is now apparent that the Chinese had brought at least two field armies into the war, and the moves of one side versus the other would portend a lengthy and indecisive battle. As time went on, the Chinese would assemble and move nine armies into the peninsula. They were successful because their units moved mostly at night under strict discipline and thus were not observed by UN air reconnaissance.

The reports of the fighting, along with the increase in casualties flowing back to the hospitals, confirmed clearly that the Chinese support offered to the North Koreans, under whatever guise, was indeed real and deadly and was fast becoming a critical element in the war. The resistance of the North Koreans stiffened, and frequent counterattacks against our forces were initiated. It is quite likely that the irregulars who ambushed us were used as a spearhead force for some of these attacks.

The UN command had been split at this point. In the western sector, Walker still retained control of the Eighth Army, which comprised the I and IX corps. In the eastern sector, General Almond commanded the X Corps. Each command had been given attack orders to drive north toward the Yalu River. Perhaps because of the race north and the Communists' fear that UN forces would secure all of Korea, causing the puppet regime of Kim Il Sung to collapse, the Chinese offered assistance to North Korea and committed the People's Liberation Army (PLA) to stop the advance.

The next two weeks were a success story for UN forces. The narrow neck of the peninsula, stretching between Kaesong on the west and Wonsan on the east, allowed our forces to continue their attacks toward the Yalu. While these were undoubtedly coordinated by the UN command, the race for the river appeared to have become a personal goal of the division commanders making the attacks. On the eastern front the 17th Regimental Combat Team swept toward the Manchurian border and by November 21 had reached the Yalu at Hyesangin. This RCT was a sister regiment of the one I had been with in Japan. Shortly after, the 1st Marine Division's lead elements were near the Chosin Reservoir along with other units of the 7th Division. In the western sector, I Corps was moving steadily toward Sinuiji on the Yalu.

In the center, the 24th RCT and her sister regiments of the 25th Division moved forward toward Unsan. All of these towns appeared to be significant strongpoints to be held while negotiations to end the war were established. The real tragedy of the operation was our failure to believe the Chinese would enter the war en masse. It was not an easy time for the 24th. As the regiment moved north, any number of ambushes were directed at friendly patrols. Sister regiments also were attacked. North Korean forces, realizing the greater strength of our troops, were instructed to harass and strike wherever and whenever they could find targets behind the lines. Their objective was to wait for the Chinese to come into the fight.

By November 20 the Chinese had crossed the Yalu River in force and were attacking south against the 25th Division with well-seasoned frontline troops. About this time the 24th had moved into the Yong-byon area as part of a limited offensive with the 35th Regiment. Task Force Dolvin, which was to spearhead the operation north, met heavy enemy resistance. My battalion and other units were added to the task force to give it more strength. On Thanksgiving Day the 24th was committed against a strong and determined enemy force, but during the next several days the entire division was forced to withdraw in the face of the Chinese offensive. By the end of the month the fortunes of war had changed drastically, and the 24th, along with its fellow regiments, was on

Pres. Syngman Rhee of the Republic of Korea talks to the citizens of Wonsan, November 22, 1950. *U.S. Army photograph*

the roads headed south. Again, as in the months before, the 24th and other units were moving backward in an attempt to slow the Red hordes before them.

On November 28, MacArthur's headquarters issued Communique 14, which reported: "Enemy reactions developed in the course of our assault actions of the past four days disclose that a major segment of the Chinese continental armed forces in Army, Corps, and Divisional organization of an aggregate strength of over 200,000 men is now arrayed against the United Nations forces in North Korea. There exists the obvious intent and preparation for support of these forces by heavy reinforcements now concentrated in the privileged sanctuary north of the international boundary and constantly moving forward. Consequently, we face an entirely new war."

Major counterattacks developed toward the end of November, shortly after a limited offensive was launched by the UN forces.

Burning village of Sibyon-ni, as UN forces give ground under Chinese assault, December 10, 1950. *U.S. Army photograph*

The first Chinese field army hit the western sector with increased frequency, fully determined to break the back of the UN offensive. Then a second Chinese field army attacked with full strength against the UN's eastern flank. It was indeed, as MacArthur said, a new war. The UN command's attempt to terminate hostilities and to reach a peaceful settlement had been foiled. The clash between the two great armies placed negotiations on hold.

Winter was now upon Korea. The icy winds and snow descended on the two opposing armies. December brought freezing weather, and injuries and disabilities due to the cold started to take their toll. The withdrawals were accomplished as they had been the summer before. One RCT would hold while another passed through its position, pull back, and then hold again until successive defense lines were established by the division and fortified for a more determined stand.

Five lines were initially designated, but as the Chinese pushed forward and flanked the division's forces on the east as it occupied Line Able, the 24th and 35th RCTs went into position on Line Baker along the Imjin River. The river offered a natural obstacle to the onrushing Chinese. But by launching another powerful offensive, the Chinese penetrated the division's right flank again. Then the orders were given to fall back to a new line designated for the defense of Seoul. By the end of December the entire Eighth Army had moved to this line. But the Chinese were not to be denied their prize, the capital city. Continuing the attack, they penetrated or overran the lines, with the net result that all UN forces were ordered to withdraw across the frozen Han River.

Once again, our troops were being driven back by great masses of human waves rolling in like breakers against a beach. In the eastern sector, the Chosin Reservoir was surrounded, and men fought desperately to extricate themselves from the hordes that came upon them. The 1st Marine and the 7th Infantry divisions fought their way through the Chinese army to meet with the 3d Infantry, which drove north from the Hungnam beachhead to give them some relief.

After they were freed from the encircling trap, they evacuated by sea and escaped being slaughtered. This was an American Dunkirk, a rather sad chapter in the war. Facing four Chinese field armies, units in the western sector attempted to fight delaying actions, but they too were overwhelmed by the troops coming against them and were forced to withdraw to the south. The Chinese drew heavy casualties; their commanders were immune to or indifferent to the cold and loss of life. Seoul fell for the second time in six months. Finally, south of the Han River, the retreat stopped. The UN forces reorganized and regrouped, licked their wounds, and dug in for a defensive stand. They would not initiate another offensive until spring.

So the allied offensive came to a halt, and there was little news that wasn't depressing, to say the least. The month of December was grim; the stories we read were not very upbeat. The UN forces kept being pushed south, and one defeat after another made the headlines. In the comfort of the hospital I felt empathy for the soldiers and often wondered what was happening to the 24th Infantry and the men who had been with me as we started north. The reports were generally of major fighting actions, and I had no news about individual units and how they were faring in the brutal weather that had descended on Korea. Periodically, I would hear that a friend had been killed or wounded; usually the news was from someone who had become a casualty himself and was now in the hospital.

Tanks enter Seoul as UN forces withdraw to set up new positions, December 27, 1950. *U.S. Army photograph*

One day I heard that a friend of mine, Bruce Wallace, was one of many lost during the fighting in North Korea. He and I had served together at Fort Benning and had shared many good times in Georgia. I knew that he was with the 7th Infantry, and I contacted them when I was told that he had been lost. I received a cryptic answer to my inquiry. It read in part: "Lt. Wallace was a member of Company 'G', 7th Infantry, A.P.O. 468. He is officially listed as MIA [Missing in Action]; however, unofficially, I have been told he was killed. He was lost on 3 December 1950 at Huksu-ri, a small village between Hamhung and the Chosin Reservoir. His body was never recovered; hence, his being carried MIA, but another officer who was present states that Lt. Wallace was dead when they were forced to withdraw, and they were only able to remove the wounded." Only recently have I learned that Wallace was not killed as reported.

I guess one should steel oneself to the brutality and deadliness of war and all that it brings, but the young have resiliency that gives them the chance to recover quickly, and I was able to shed my sorrow temporarily and get on with my life.

Several weeks later I was transferred to the 172nd Station Hospital in Sendai. Sendai had been my first posting when I arrived in Japan. I had stopped only long enough to get assignment orders and had renewed acquaintances with several friends from the States. Sendai was the headquarters of the 7th Infantry Division. At the outset of the Korean War it had been stripped of many of its troops (I was one of them), but after it was reequipped and brought up to personnel strength, it had been deployed as part of MacArthur's invasion at Inchon.

I was pleasantly surprised to find that some of my friends had not been sent home. I fully expected that with the war in Korea, the DACs, many of whom had brought specific skills to assist the Japanese to get back on their feet, would have been sent to the States. Several came to the hospital, and when I was given convalescent leave, I went home with them. The army was quite flexible and generous with those of us who were on leave. Other than being required to report in periodically, we were permitted to do what we wanted.

During my stay there, one other memorable incident occurred. I was sitting in the post exchange one day with another lieutenant who had been in my class at the infantry school. Rutland Beard and I had trained together there, and he was one of my friends who had been assigned to Japan. He was on leave for a few days from Korea but was scheduled to return the following day. His wife, Lucille, was on the verge of delivering their first baby. As a married officer, Beard had been allowed to bring his wife to Japan earlier. He wanted desperately to see his firstborn before he shipped out and had asked the doctor that morning if there was any chance of expediting the process. The medic had prescribed a large bottle of castor oil, and as we sat together, his wife would take a drink of the oil and then wash it down with orange soda. The stuff was ghastly, but like all good soldiers, she was willing to give it a whirl. It worked. A son was born the next day before Rutland had to catch his flight, and he had the good fortune to see the baby. Whether it was the castor oil or a Divine Hand in the matter, he will never know.

Shortly thereafter, I was allowed out of the hospital on leave. Tokyo was an exciting place, crowded with humanity, an endless flow and counterflow of people going every direction in subways, buses, taxis, and elevated expressways. There was little trace of the fire bombings of World War II that had wiped out or severely damaged much of the city. It had resurrected itself out of the ashes, and the people of this country were going about their lives as if there were no occupation or a war next door. The flashing neon signs and lights and sounds gave the city the look and feel of Christmas, as though this were a national holiday of the Japanese. Tokyo has been called the glitter capital of the world because of the profusion of neon signs, and I could see why. The Ginza, the city's premier shopping district, was alive with crowds of shoppers, and everything about the place reminded me of the Christmas season.

The year before, I had met a Japanese family. They had invited me into their home, and we had become friends. It had been my first in-depth exposure to the Japanese culture, and I was made a part of the festivities held at the end of the year to celebrate the new year. The celebration extended for a period of some days, during which time special foods were prepared and gifts exchanged, and I felt quite privileged to be a part of the festival. They were surprised when I showed up now at their door. They could not do enough for me. They treated me royally, and I was happy to be with them.

In the middle of February 1951 I received orders to return to Korea. I had expected the reassignment much earlier, but it still was unwelcome news, and I was less than excited about the prospect of going back. There were no options available; my time-out had ended. Along the line I was given movement orders to travel south through Honshu to Sasebo, the gateway to Korea. On February 23, after traveling for nearly a week, I reported to the 1st Battalion of the 24th.

11. Call It Homecoming

I cannot recall where the battalion was located when I rejoined it. The headquarters may have been in the vicinity of Kumjongni, but that is just a guess. I know that it was south of the Han River in a defensive position. This was the line that had been established after the previous general withdrawal of UN forces. Returning to combat after having been wounded and separated from a unit for some time requires far more than just the physical move. I had to prepare myself mentally for the reunion with the troops, and it was not an easy task. I did not have any exhilarating thoughts about seeing action again; I would far rather have stayed in Japan in some training job. But one's options are limited, and a soldier's personal needs or desires must of necessity be subordinate to the needs of the service.

I do not remember the processing route that I traveled, but I suspect that I was sent from one replacement depot to another on my return trip. When I finally reached the battalion's command post, I hauled my gear from the jeep and dismounted. Several men from the headquarters staff recognized me and welcomed me back. I looked at the few who had appeared before me and noted how fit they seemed to be, certainly not like the ragtag men I had left behind. They looked sharp and rested and well dressed. It was a contrast from what I expected. But then I too was in clean clothes and had shaved.

As a senior lieutenant, I had hoped to get a company to command, but I had no knowledge about the personnel levels or the status of any unit in the battalion. I guessed that I would be assigned wherever there was an opening, and if a company commander was needed, I would get the slot. I was excited about the prospects, but at the same time I felt I could do a good job on a staff. I did not expect to get my old platoon back. It was not "my" platoon in any case. Someone would have taken my place, either the platoon sergeant or some new replacement second lieutenant. Still, I wanted to see the men again, to see for myself how many of the old gang were still hanging in there waiting for their chance to get out of Korea. As soon as I could get to them, I decided I would go.

I was aware of the men watching as I walked across the compound. The CP tent was the largest shelter in the area, surrounded by other smaller tents that housed various and sundry people and things. There were few vehicles scattered around, but my focus was on the tent looming before me. The weather was clear and cold, and the sun was shining strong. I felt the cold even as I walked, but the chill was not from the weather but from the fear of not knowing how I would be met or what my next assignment would be. It was not the fear of combat again, but the kind of anxiety I had experienced before the ambush, of my inability to know what lay ahead. I took a deep breath and reached for the flap that served as the door of the tent.

The first person I saw was the battalion's S-2, or intelligence officer, Capt. Gus Gillert, who looked up and then reached out and grabbed my hand. He greeted me as though I had just returned from the dead. Then others of the staff welcomed me warmly, telling me they were glad to see me back, joshing me about having a long vacation, and kidding me about missing all the fighting. Their genuine concern made me feel good, and whatever negative thoughts I had entertained about returning quickly vanished.

The camaraderie of men in a combat unit, I believe, is not shared in any other profession. There is complete unity of purpose, a sharing of hardship and success, of understanding and forgiveness. However close other organizations may become in terms of overall objectives to be met or roles that must be played, I do not think men and women share the same bases that allow for the singleness of purpose that is found here. A military organization enjoins us to have pride and esprit de corps, to serve or work together for a common cause, and we come together as a cohesive group to hold these truths. There is nothing dramatic about this common bonding, nor is it patriotic gesturing; it is simply a way of life that we accept.

Several new faces looked me over or just introduced themselves and went back to their labors. Soon the word circulated among them that I was one of the early veterans who had been wounded, and I was given a lot of respect. The fact that I had been gone so long and then returned gave me a bit of celebrity status, which I enjoyed.

When I was able to talk to the battalion commander, I was pleased to find it was Major Baranowski. If I remember correctly,

Baranowski had joined the 1st Battalion sometime later in the war, but I had known him as a fine officer who had a lot of smarts and grit. I liked him, and we had gotten along well together. He told me I would not be returning to my platoon, and without further discussion assigned me as the assistant operations officer (S-3). I would be working with Gus again, and I was happy with the assignment.

At different times during the Korean War, Captain Gillert acted as both a combined S-2/S-3 or held the jobs separately. Gillert was a solid, well-trained officer, and we got along great. He and I had worked together from the beginning, and I was probably closer to him than anyone else in the battalion. Although he was senior to me, he never pulled rank or tried to be superior. We thought a lot alike, which made our working relationship easy.

The position of the operations officer (S-3) is that of formulating and implementing the tactical plans of an operation at the lowest level. Generally, the division lays out the strategy for a particular operation and then passes it down the line to the regiments and battalions. The commanders turn to the S-3, who then assumes the job of establishing the operational plans requisite for carrying out the commander's orders. In brief, he is responsible for establishing the direction and scope of the actions to be taken by the fighting units, the companies and platoons that will take the fight to the enemy.

The operations officer must know the troop dispositions and strengths and use them to advantage. He establishes the objectives, the method of attack, the departure times, and the supporting units to be deployed to assist in the fight. The "3" has to work closely with the intelligence officer or "2"; while their areas of expertise are separate, overlapping information is important to each. The "2" will assess the enemy's dispositions and strength and feed this info to the S-3, and together they will come up with possible counteractions that can be used if the situation arises.

In my judgment, the G-3 (operations officer at the division level) or S-3 (operations officer at the regimental or battalion level) is the single staff officer who has to know the big picture. He works closely with every staff officer and must know how and when to use the administrative and logistical support available. Of course, without the support of every staff member he cannot be very effective. Several years before, I had worked as a sergeant on the 82d Airborne Division's staff, so I was quite familiar with the work to be done.

The assignment would prove to be exciting, and I was thrilled to get the post.

I soon learned of the actions that had occurred while I was gone. After the Chinese entered the war and instituted massed human-wave attacks, a general withdrawal was ordered and went into effect across the UN line. December appeared to be a repetition of the previous summer days when delay, withdrawal, delay was the rule. On December 23, General Walker was killed in a vehicle accident similar to the one that had taken the life of his patron and mentor, General Patton, five years earlier. Walker had been replaced by Gen. Matthew Ridgway, who brought to the Eighth Army an instant rejuvenation and optimism. Ridgway was to become known as a soldier's soldier; there was never any doubt in our minds that he was a superior commander in every way.

During January the Chinese PLAs continued their offensive. The threat of enveloping attacks by the enemy on extended division sectors precipitated a withdrawal of UN forces. Ridgway's headquarters issued orders again, with the net result that the 25th Division regiments withdrew from Seoul, allowing the Communists to take control of the city. Somewhere around Chonan, the division units stopped and set up defensive positions. The battalion had been bloodied during the retreat, but as soon as it licked its wounds, another offensive action was ordered. Initially, it was a time of limited probing actions, principally that of sending out patrols to determine enemy strengths and intentions. In fact, it was the prelude for another UN offensive called Operation Thunderbolt.

The 24th was assigned the task of providing protection for the MSR between Chonan and Taejon. Enemy soldiers roamed throughout the area, and pitched battles erupted periodically. By the end of January, the division implemented Thunderbolt and advanced in columns of regimental strength through Suwon on the main axis toward Seoul. Then it moved on to secure the Inchon-Yongdongpo area and prepared for a rapid breakout to the north.

By the time I arrived on the scene, the division had been shifted east to the area occupied by the 1st Cavalry Division and was ordered to move forward to the south bank of the Han River. It had consolidated and built up fortifications against strong enemy thrusts, and having done so, it was in position to launch still another offensive action when higher headquarters gave the signal to go.

Baranowski wanted me to get involved right away with the planning activities for the coming offensive, which he believed would

Men from 77th Engineer Company (C), sweeping for mines along a road, February 13, 1951. *U.S. Army photograph*

be the river-crossing assault. I quickly read up on the current situation. Elements of the division were attacking north on a wide front, while other UN forces were on our left flank heading north as well. I believe this was the fourth time in eight months that we were making an all-out effort to gain ground, much of which we had unfortunately covered before.

While there continued to be successes, the Communists were not quite ready to call it a day, and so for the most part the infantry had to slug it out mile by mile as the friendly units inched forward. Tank-infantry teams spearheaded the drive and offered greater mobility than we had experienced before. We had used armor previously, but the "ground pounders" still had to assault the hills to prevent enemy reinforcements. The combined tactical use of both capabilities kept the Communists off-stride and unable to launch massed attacks.

One of the major problems we faced was again the flow of

the native Koreans as they moved with the tides of war. The road and rail networks placed the same constraints on them as on us, and it seemed that whenever we moved forward or backward, the refugees followed. Now as we moved north, so too did the people. Near the town of Sam Jang Dong, shortly after my return, we encountered another large group heading north. I watched them one morning, men and women and children trudging wearily from the village toward our frontline positions. Whether they would find a place to stop at the end of the day was uncertain, but a strong force was pulling them, some beckoning light that called them to their roots.

They had become nomads in their own land. They gave the appearance of Gypsies, but there were none among them who could tell what fortunes or misfortunes they might encounter on their return. They had traveled across the barren, snow-covered mountain ridges or through the passes to find a deserted village and then had stayed with us during the night. They cooked their meager rations and rolled into heavy comforters to sleep until dawn, the music of supporting artillery fire giving them a restless night.

Then they were on their way again. The men and boys carried the heavier loads, balanced precariously upon the homemade A frames. The women and young girls trailed behind, walking erectly. Some carried babies on their backs, but all had earthenware containers perched on their heads. For warmth against the cold, they wore probably all the clothes they owned – fur caps and long coats and ragged skirts, and most of them had tattered socks covering their feet.

I could not help but feel sorry for the lot, for they were setting out in the poorest of weather with inadequate clothing and probably not enough calories to keep them warm. They did not speak to us; they had become immune to the adversities of their environment interrupted by soldiers from another land. I thought, "What hope can they have? What dreams can they share?" As I watched them leave, I wondered what gave them the strength to carry on. How could they survive the war and the hopelessness it brought to them? How had they managed to survive all these months in strange surroundings and with few necessities? I think they must have had great resilience, and maybe a good measure of perseverance thrown in as well.

Toward the end of the month rumors were flying that another new, strong offensive was in the mill. Our location on the Han River made it appear likely that we would play a major role. There was a lot of work ahead to sort out the details if we were to be involved. When we had retraced our steps the third time north, we had moved slowly and with care, not wanting to stretch our logistics train or the communications links. We maintained close contact with sister units. We had learned not to allow penetrations between the assigned areas.

Heavy artillery fire and close air support had been used on enemy troop concentrations, and when we had to withdraw, long-range bombers picked up the beat and showered tons of munitions on enemy men and equipment day and night. The coordination of land, sea, and air power clearly demonstrated that a modern army could move forward, deal with a superior force, and withdraw in an orderly fashion. The lessons had sometimes been hard, and in some cases shocking, but we had become a better-trained, more powerful force in every way. This time every unit would be in place. It would be well equipped, heavily supported, and ready to fight. I believe we were determined – and mad.

12. The Han River Crossing

During the cold months of January and February there appeared to be a tendency to dig in and recoup our losses. Aggressive patrol actions were ordered, however, and the Eighth Army initiated another offensive. This action, while partially successful, had limited results. Supplies now had been accumulated for a major thrust north, and Ridgway decided the time was ripe for attack. My guess is that the plan evolved from learning that a Chinese offensive was in the offing. Ridgway had two options. He could sit tight and wait for an attack, or he could take the offensive. He chose the latter.

It was the beginning of Operation Ripper, a coordinated attack across the Han River. The 25th Division was ordered to make the crossing with all regiments in line, assaulting three major mountains on the north side where Chinese army troops were firmly entrenched. Other UN forces would attack along the line. It would be the third major offensive move of the war. The operations order probably read in part: "25th Infantry Division, with attachments, makes assault crossing of Han River and attacks north in zone, by successive phase lines, to seize and secure Line ———. Prepare to continue attack on order to Line ———. Turkish Brigade protects corps right flank." Whatever its composition, the short paragraph carried the larger implication that for the first time in the Korean War an assault river crossing would be mounted.

The wheels were set in motion. As they turned, geared for the landing on the north bank, the collection and evaluation of both friendly and hostile information commenced. I remember tremendous planning was required, because we had about a week's notice. The intelligence team from division and regiment started to grind out information on the Chinese order of battle: who was defending, what units, their defensive positions, and a host of other matters. The logistics of the operation were horrendous: the requirements for vehicles, assault boats, engine support, ammo, rations, water, gasoline, medical supplies, and so on. All were critical and had to be requisitioned, received, and stored until the attack. Everything was critical to the success of the operation.

As soon as the information was available to the infantry battalions (the spokes of the wheels), we started to write the battalions operations order for our own units. Our section, S-3, had to describe and provide direction to commanders, in which we spelled out the tasks and objectives, enemy and friendly situation, the mission, how the attack would be executed, and what subordinate commanders could expect in terms of logistical and communications support. All of this was supplemented by staff meetings and briefings for the offensive.

The operations order is probably the single most important order issued by a commander. The receipt of our order from regimental headquarters brought some excitement, because we had been sitting on the south bank of the river for some time and had speculated where and when the crossing would be made and who would participate. The regimental S-3 called the initial meeting, and as the planning progressed, we set up our own briefings. The events are as I recorded them.

"D-Day minus 2. The weather is cool and clear, and the sun has melted the half inch of snow which gave us a white, glittering dawn. To all outward appearance, it is more than another routine day. There is excitement in the air, sensed by everyone. Other regimental combat teams have been moving forward from assembly areas in the rear. The artillery, for both general and direct support, has displaced and moved into new positions for the crossing. 'Long Toms' [8-inch guns] have moved up, not only to bolster the artillery fire, but to give confidence to those making the crossing.

"The battalions have received the written order and planning is well underway. Engineers, tankers, communications specialists are covering the details with the staff. Nothing is too small to discuss. There will be no dry runs, only a first, wet and hot run.

"Fox will cross on the right flank, Easy on the left. Section of machine guns attached to each assault company. George, as reserve, will cross on CO's order [Fox, Easy, and George are infantry companies from the 2d Battalion]. How many boats? Twenty assault boats per company. Engineers will bring them to assembly point. Tanks will initially support attack from south bank."

The briefings continued hour after hour, giving instructions, receiving comments, and discussing details of the operation. The intelligence officer gave information on the enemy forces, the adjutant designated reporting procedures, the medical officer told where the collecting points for the wounded would be located, and the supply officer addressed the logistical support and spelled out the priorities for ammunition, gas, and rations. My notes reflect the whole process:

> The basic load for individual and crew-served weapons must be carried across with the assault waves. . . . 50-ton raft and foot bridge will be constructed as soon as possible. . . . You must take enough with you to sustain yourselves the first few hours. . . . It must be clear in everyone's mind that nothing must be left to chance or guess.
>
> As detailed planning evolves from the staff meetings, the men who will be in the assault waves commence training on river crossings and cold-wet weather operations. In the assembly areas the assault craft, flat-bottom plywood boats capable of carrying nine men with equipment and a crew of three, are man-handled, loaded, unloaded, and reloaded again. There are dry runs and still more dry runs. The patrols are out, probing and feinting along the enemy lines. They draw fire and direct and adjust artillery on the suspected positions before returning. Their purpose: to harass, confuse, and throw the Chinese forces off-guard.
>
> The war does not stop with darkness. There are a myriad of details to clarify. Maps, aerial photographs, and reports from our observation posts are collated and analyzed. The night deepens. Another day has been devoted to correcting or altering the final decisions of the planning. Men in the assembly area are trying to sleep, fully aware that it might be days before they can sleep again. The night is cold and black. The stars shed only a faint light. Breakfast is a hot meal of eggs, cereal, toast and coffee, little more than a midnight snack.
>
> D-Day 7 March.
>
> 0230 hours. Assault battalion departs assembly area. The only noise is a dull thudding sound as boot heels strike the frozen ground. Now and then, a stifled cough is heard. Men are moving mechanically, loaded with ammunition and rations, some to their death.
>
> 0400 hours. Battalion closed in position assembly area on south bank of river. Men have been briefed and are getting last-minute instructions. Basic loads of ammo are rechecked, and commanders asked to review assignments. The waiting has begun. Some men are sitting and dozing, while others stare into nowhere. Close your eyes, soldier, against the hell that will soon come.
>
> 0600 hours. Observation posts are manned and prepared. Staff officers are waiting, counting off the minutes. Then . . .
>
> 0615 hours. H-Hour. Assault waves are beginning the crossing after carrying boats from assembly area to the beaches. There is little confusion; the hours of planning and rehearsal are paying off.
>
> 0635 hours. Both assault companies have completed crossing under heavy mortar and automatic weapons fire and are moving from the beach.

Medics of the 24th Infantry carry a wounded man back to an aid station, February 16, 1951. *U.S. Army photograph*

0645 hours. It appears as if nothing could live through the hell of what appears to be the heaviest concentration of artillery ever assembled in this war – 146 guns, including those of the Royal Artillery, are throwing shells out as quickly as the guns can be reloaded. Tanks, too, add their weight as the 90-mm guns start to pound the ground north of the river. Both 4.2-inch and 81-mm mortars are slamming round after round, lending still more fire and flame against the mountain, now rearing its darkened mass in the dull grey of morning. Quad .50-caliber machine guns and 40-mm cannon are raking the terrain savagely, their tracer ammo lighting up the deeper shadows of the mountain. It is a scene from Dante's hell.

0710 hours. The enemy forces are reacting slowly after the intense preparatory firing. As the front-line companies move forward, they begin to receive sporadic 120-mm and 82-mm mortar fire. From the northwest, small arms and automatic weapons commence firing. On the bridgehead the companies are now actively engaged in the fight before them.

Men of the 24th RCT rest on a hill near the Han River during Operation Ripper, March 7, 1951. *U.S. Army photograph*

0800 hours. Fox Company has reached its objective and is attempting to organize its position.

0945 hours. Easy Company, after meeting enemy resistance varying from moderately stiff to heavy, has seized its objective.

1010 hours. The foot bridge and ferry site are being subjected to sporadic mortar fire, the intent to dissuade the engineers from working. They get the message and stop for the moment. [Some time later, the shelling on the ferry site stopped, and the engineers commenced working to get the bridge-raft set up and ready to transport the tanks to the north bank of the river.]

1145 hours. George Company has crossed on the CO's order and is attacking north on the left flank of Easy Company.

1300 hours. First Company of third battalion is moving across the river to protect right flank of Fox Company. King Company will secure the river in vicinity of 50-ton ferry site.

1600 hours. George Company secures objective and has begun to organize for the night.

It has been an endless, tiring day. The bridgehead is being
held; for the moment we can be proud of that. But for the ground
we have gained, we've lost some fine men. As usual, the dirty
work of digging out the Chinese becomes the exclusive job of the
infantry troops. During the day, as we watched the air strikes, we
thought the job would be easier. The jets and the Mustangs flashed
from the sky like hawks after their prey. The planes clobbered the
Chinese with 5-inch rockets and 20-mm cannon fire. They
dropped napalm and high explosive bombs and then, for good
measure, raked the ground with machine-gun fire. The air force
did a tremendous job, and many Chinese were burned or blown
out of their holes. But for all who died today for Chairman Mao or
some other false god, there were many others who dug in deeper,
and after the planes had finished plastering them, came out of
their hole to give us hell again.

There was a lot of time spent looking for stragglers who had
been bypassed as the ground troops moved forward to their objectives. When discovered, they were quickly captured and escorted
to the rear.

In the early afternoon, when the ferry was ready to accept vehicles, I took the first jeep across with the first tank. I cannot remember what my mission was except to check out the ferry and
see if it was ready for general use. When we arrived on the north
side and unloaded at the river's edge, I cautioned the driver that
I would lead the way in the tank up to the road, which was above
us at the base of the mountain. I was about twenty-five yards ahead
of the jeep, looking carefully for mines, when the driver decided
to go another direction.

At the sound of a mighty explosion, I turned to see the jeep
disintegrating before my eyes. It had struck a mine and was flying
apart in every direction, the bodies of the two men with it. Fortunately, all vehicles had sandbags placed on the floor under the driver
and passenger; this reduced the force of the blast, and while the
men were wounded, they were not killed.

About the same time, we started to draw fire from a bypassed
hole to the left. I knew that sometimes there would be more than
one person in an underground bunker. Running back to the tank,
I directed the gunner to destroy the hole. He fired once. It was a
direct hit by the 90-mm gun, and the bunker erupted in flames.
Whether it was a lucky shot or not, I don't know. But that was the
end of the sniping fire.

My notes continue:

After a few hours spent directing fresh troops into position, I re-crossed the river for the night. It got cold quickly, and as darkness fell, we realized how completely the river separated units. The night wore on, but few men slept. There was always the fear of a coun-terattack, so we sat and waited for the next phase of the operation.

2030 hours. The first heavy tanks are moving across on the raft. The blackout adds to the difficulty of landing them. The cold night is endless for us, and it is far from over.

0330 hours. The Chinese are counterattacking from the northwest, frantically driving and pushing to dislodge us from the north bank. Strength is estimated to be a reinforced battalion.

0500 hours. Easy and Fox Companies have been pushed back badly. They have now lost 1,500 yards, and the pressure is strong.

1030 hours. The artillery and mortars continue to fire in sup-port of the line companies, and as the infantry digs in, the action appears to be contained.

1100 hours. King Company is now attacking east of Fox Com-pany against resistance which is moderate to heavy. The number of enemy dead is estimated to be high.

1400 hours. Another company is crossing. Love Company moves quickly to get into position before dark.

1800 hours. Dark has fallen, and the battle has been punish-ing throughout the day. The battalion has now regained 1,200 yards. Everyone is exhausted in mind and body.

The intelligence officer briefs us again: "Estimated enemy strength which can be employed in our sector is one regiment rein-forced with armor. He can attack at any time and can reinforce with troops from the Seoul area. Or he can delay with successive positions along our axis or withdraw to defensive positions on the high ground north of the Seoul-Masagiri road." The advantages are the enemy's; we will respond as is necessary in order to keep the pressure on. What will the enemy force do?

2230 hours. The enemy is partially disengaging, leaving de-laying forces on the high ground. The immediate threat of further counterattacks has passed. The offensive will continue.

0759 hours. Officially, dawn. The artillery and mortar fire sup-port, which has continued all night, becomes more intense in order to cover the attacking troops. The 2d Battalion reaches and se-cures its objective. Platoon-sized armor-infantry patrols are formed and alerted for action.

1410 hours. Patrols advancing northwest are engaging approx-imately three companies of Chinese. Again the enemy force suffers heavy casualties before withdrawing to the northeast.

Troops move up once again, past a dead Chinese soldier, following the Han River crossing. *U.S. Army photograph*

With control of the commanding ground and having reached successive phase lines, the bridgehead is ours. Three discouraging days and two endless nights have finally resulted in a temporary victory. The fighting was hard; the troops fought tenaciously to gain and hold a mile or less of mountain terrain. The 2d Battalion was given a rest, and the 1st Battalion passed through them to continue the attack.

Along the twisted railroad tracks, astride the road, and even on the mountain the dead lay, mute testimony to the great losses suffered by the Chinese. Grotesque headless and limbless defenders were sprawled everywhere. The Chinese who survived, many bleeding from ears and noses from the ruptures caused by the concussions of artillery against their holes, stumbled along under guard, unaware of the significance of the battle. It was the largest group of prisoners captured by any division in any one day since the Chinese had entered the war. Now they were shocked and weary and out of the fighting. It was my first sight of Chinese soldiers, and I was somewhat impressed by their clothing and equipment. They all looked to be young boys – but then most of us looked the same.

By crossing southeast of Seoul, we forced a withdrawal from the city. The Chinese thought it could not be done, certainly not at this place, but we had proven otherwise. It had been a tough fight, but there were tougher ones ahead. When one hill was taken, there was always another standing defiantly in the distance to be taken the same way. Few in the infantry walked across Korea. They crawled and dug their fingernails through the stinking mud of the rice paddies and across the barren mountain ridges, hand-over-hand, capturing a bit of land before being forced to give it up again.

The Han River assault crossing was the first. It would be followed by the Imjin, the Hantan, and others. It was only a small chapter of the war, but for us, it will be hard to forget.

13. Thrust and Counterthrust

After crossing the Han, the division's forward troops were ordered to move slowly and to thrust north against the enemy. This time, however, the command did not allow the individual units to burst forth in pursuit but ordered a halt when one unit was slowed because of heavy resistance in its sector. When the opposition had been cleared – which sometimes required hours of waiting – then all units moved forward again in line. Combat units also were provided with supporting troops. Tankers, engineer units, and supply specialists provided depth behind the lines, and no single frontline unit could have wished for anything better. There is no question but that this decision to move slowly, and at the same time to protect adjacent flanks, was a wise one.

On Easter Sunday, March 25, we were still slogging northwest. It had rained hard, and the water raced down from the hills and turned the ground into a clay quagmire, making our forward progress more difficult. Our units and troops of the Turkish Brigade continued to move forward, and by April 10 they had driven the Chinese forces back to the Hantan River. For a few days the action waned as the enemy reorganized in order to get ready for a spring counterthrust.

During the lull I decided one day to make a liaison visit to the Turkish Brigade headquarters. I do not remember how far away it was located, but I do recall that it was a beautiful spring day and that the sun was shining as we arrived. It was time for a picnic. As soon as we dismounted from the jeep, the brigade commander met us and invited us to lunch. Tables had been arranged in front of the mess tent, and they were covered with dozens of mess kits and metal trays overflowing with food. The ubiquitous C rations had been dumped in many of the trays, and there were other foods in the rations for the Turks that we did not have in ours. There were stacks of fresh, round loaves of bread that made my mouth water. When chow call was announced, the men went to the table armed with spoons, and then to my surprise and shock they started around the tables of smorgasbord dipping their spoons into first

Men of the 77th Engineer Company (C) blasting the Chinese out of caves and bunkers along the Hantan River, April 11, 1951. *U.S. Army photograph*

one dish and then another, eating each spoonful before going on to the next. I figured when in Turkey, do what the Turks do, and I too dug into the feast spread before me.

A few days later intelligence sources reported that heavy enemy troop concentrations were being formed for an imminent attack to be initiated about April 20. An alert was issued to all units immediately. It was suspected or reported that the Chinese intended to launch an attack to catch us bogged down in the mud and washed-out roads. At the time, we were located just south of Choriwon on relatively high ground. That fact, however, did not apply to the support forces, which of necessity were confined to the valley floor, where the weather did have an effect on the mobility of all units. The destroyed cities of Choriwon and Yonchon, the latter one near the place we had been ambushed, formed the anchor for a strongly defended main line of resistance for the Chinese.

This was where the Chinese and North Korean reorganization was being put together. Since we had fought over the same ground before, I was not very excited about renewing old memories. But such is war, and we had to move on.

Because enemy troop concentrations had been identified, intelligence gathering quickly became a priority action. Both division and regimental staffs wanted updated information about the enemy to enable them to start planning their tactical moves. As the assistant S-3, I decided the best way to get information was to fly over the forward battle areas and assess the situation from the air. I thought that in this way I could get a picture of what was happening along the front. On April 20 and 21, I requested air reconnaissance flights in a light observation plane.

The division air section happily agreed. As an observer, I occupied the rear seat, and from my perch I was able to see clearly what was happening below. It was easy to discern our frontline positions, both from the alignment of the foxholes and from the colored panel markers designating the forward battle line of the units. As we flew along, I could see exploding artillery rounds in the distance, from either interdiction or just plain harassing fire to keep the Chinese off-balance.

In midafternoon on the second day, we were flying forward of friendly lines a few miles. I was scanning the ground carefully for any sign of troops or equipment dumps when I spotted what looked like a battalion of Chinese moving generally south toward our lines. It was a startling sight.

I immediately called to the pilot and asked for his opinion of the size of the unit. He couldn't estimate it, but we both knew it was large. I asked him to go around again and to fly a bit lower so that I could try to get a better look.

I could see them clearly now. They were jogging along in full daylight in a column that extended for some distance to the rear, about four or five men abreast, seemingly oblivious to the fact that an observation plane was circling overhead. My guess was that the band consisted of about six hundred to one thousand men moving toward our lines. At the rate they were moving, I estimated they would be there sometime during the night. I reached for the radio to notify headquarters and made immediate contact. I told HQ the size of the Chinese force and its expected arrival time at the front and asked for an air strike.

We made a few more circles to check out some other locations and then returned to the strip and landed. As soon as I returned to battalion, we reviewed the situation and attempted to predict where the force would attack. I don't know whether the air force could get a strike on the target before dark, but if it did not, the combat units were in for a strong attack. One of the surprises of the war, I believe, was that both the North Koreans and the Chinese could move so quickly day or night. It was the first time that I had seen a major group moving like this. They were not loaded down with excess equipment but carried only their weapons.

Those whom we killed or captured usually had a small supply of ammunition and a rice ration but little else to slow them down. They may have carried canteens, but I cannot recall seeing many of them so equipped. They had amazing stamina and could get moving much faster than our own troops. How they managed to run for miles and then attack a fortified position with such little effort is something that defies logic, but they were coming nevertheless.

On April 21 we were alerted that a general counteroffensive could be expected during the night. Because my observation had confirmed the approach of large forces, we issued orders to all frontline units to prepare for a major attack. My notes describe subsequent events:

> At 1920 hours the attacks began. First there were small, probing attacks, to harass and find soft points in our defenses and to cover massed movements along the frontal positions. In our immediate sector there was a buildup of men directly in front of us, so we were able to meet the first assault with awesome firepower. The attack was blunted. The enemy, having received heavy casualties, withdrew to reorganize before hitting us again. As the night wore on, the troops grew weary, and the Chinese again attacked our positions. From 0200 hours until dawn the battle continued. The men fought well. The Chinese continued to throw seasoned troops into the battle, attempting to dislodge the defenders, but were unsuccessful. Shortly before dawn, regimental headquarters issued orders to withdraw.

This was getting to be old hat. We had advanced, retreated, and then started all over again. It did not sit well with those of us who had gone up and down Korea so many times. The withdrawal order that we received read: "A general withdrawal will be made commencing at dawn. . . . A series of blocking positions will be designated. . . . Units will fall back . . . in successive moves. . . and establish positions." That is exactly what happened. My notes reveal the heartache of withdrawing yet again:

Commanding officers of the B and C companies, 24th Infantry, observe firepower thrown by their companies on the west-central front, April 23, 1951. *U.S. Army photograph*

It was reminiscent of another long retreat as these men, who had fought across this strategic river, looked back and read the sign, "You are crossing the Hantan River courtesy of 1st Battalion, 24th Infantry." The faces of the men registered no bitterness, no pain, only that of total exhaustion which came after twelve-odd days of fighting. As I watched these men, so mentally and physically exhausted, retrace their steps over the ground which they had fought inch by inch to control, the wonderful words of the 23d Psalm returned, "Yea, though I walk through the valley of the shadow of death, I shall fear no evil, for Thou art with me." It was a time when men struggled for survival as they slowly shuffled along the road, and tried to cast off the bitterness of defeat.

In truth I cannot recall how many stops along the way were made or what holding positions were set up. I only know that the long march continued for several days. My notes reveal the pity of it all: "And then the dreams were shattered, and we returned to reality when a can of rations was passed to a friend, or when one glimpsed a man walking with a stick for support, as he hobbled along like a robot, impervious to the war around him. It was a time when a couple of grenades and bandoleers of ammunition weighed upon a man's shoulder mile after interminable mile, while his boots chafed blisters on his feet."

How many miles did we move? When we started, we were north of the Hantan River, which I believe was about twenty-five miles north of Seoul. Units of the regiment had gotten into position just south of Choriwon, above or north of the 38th Parallel. By the time we got back to Line Golden, we probably had covered about forty miles. It was not an easy march on several accounts: "It rained and we fought the elements as before. The men no longer ate the dust of Korea. Now the roads had turned to mud. Some had blankets and some [wore] ponchos, and some had nothing at all to protect them from the weather. The track became harder to move along. It became slippery and it was hard to gain traction. Men stumbled, cursed, cried, and kept moving."

On April 30 we moved into prepared positions on Line Golden about five miles north of Seoul. We did not know that the line had been constructed during the move north in the event we were forced to withdraw again. Some planner had recognized the potential of a Chinese field army counteroffensive, and a strong line had been created. While we had not taken a beating on this trip south and had withdrawn with few losses, the successive delaying and blocking positions had inflicted very heavy casualties on the Chinese.

It was a relief to fall into a defensive position already prepared. Chinese intelligence may have known about the defenses, or once again they may have overstrained their supply lines and could not maintain their forward momentum, but whatever the reason, they broke contact almost as soon as we settled in place. It is likely they had to regroup before thrusting into Seoul, but the UN command was having no part of it. For the next several weeks the Chinese maintained pressure on the lines and regularly threw an attack against units to probe for weak places in the lines. Skirmishes occurred across the division's front, but the men held in place. I wrote: "We stayed in place and continued to fortify our positions. The engineers delivered timbers and sandbags, and we built bunkers to strengthen the line. The men complained a lot, but there was little else to do, and it [securing the line] kept them busy and out of

Korean laborers carry supplies for UN forces up still another hill, June 18, 1951. *U. S. Army photograph*

trouble. The inclement weather continued off and on and made life uncomfortable, but it was as miserable for the Chinese as it was for us."

The only thing I remember about Line Golden was the effort to consolidate the forward positions. A Korean work force had been used originally to lay out the MLR, but they had not completed the job by the time we moved into it. The individual units laid out fields of fire, strengthened the barbed wire that had been strung, improved the bunkers, and generally tried to keep as dry as possible. Rain showers fell frequently, and it was an altogether unpleasant period. Before this time we had never been issued sandbags and lumber. So the men set about making shelters for the first time since we had arrived in Korea.

Another addition that made life easier was the antiaircraft searchlights brought forward and used to light up the night in front of the lines. I had never seen such brilliance in my life. When they were turned on, the battlefield was not nearly as frightening for the men. They would look for an enemy on the move and then bring devastating firepower on the unwelcome visitors. To what extent the searchlights had a part in destroying the Chinese forces I do not know, but their value as a psychological tool was very real for both armies.

At battalion headquarters we continued to gather intelligence on the enemy order of battle. This is a systematic search for information used to identify the enemy's units opposing friendly forces in the field. Periodically a unit would capture or pick up an enemy soldier or two, and the information provided by them would then be disseminated throughout the command. It was important to know what units were being committed and when and where. From the data collected, intelligence staffs could discern strengths and weaknesses of individual units, recognize which were seasoned troops and which were not, and even get a sense of the enemy's strategy as they moved units back and forth within the fighting zones.

Initiation of new attack planning got underway. We did not know when an offensive would be launched by UN command, but we were certainly aware that we would not sit on the line forever. About this time, we got a new battalion commander. A friend who was in Korea with me told me that during his tour, which included the time I was in the hospital, he had served under at least ten. Whatever the number, we had a high turnover in battalion commanders almost from day one. Some were wounded, mentally or physically, and were reassigned to the States or to some other unit within the 24th. Others were relieved by the regimental commander because they could not do the job required. None was killed in action that I am aware of.

The final one assigned, in my judgment, was the wrong choice at the wrong time. While he may have had solid combat experience before coming aboard, he was totally ineffective after he arrived. Again, in my opinion, the S-3 fought the battalion while the commander did precious little except bend our ears about whales.

The commander admitted to having been assigned to MacArthur's staff between 1945 and 1950, where he was responsible for, or supervised, the Japanese whaling fleet. What his specific duties were, I don't know, but on several occasions I heard him brag about his ability as a whale hunter. It seemed he accompanied the fleet and so was able to expound at length about whales in general. He knew about their mating habits and described in detail how they performed sex and what rituals preceded the consummation of the act. He could identify various species, and he could recite with conviction sizes and weights of the mammals of the deep. He knew

Members of the C Battery, 159th Field Artillery Battalion, firing 105 How-
itzer, June, 1951. *U.S. Army photograph*

a lot about whaling, but his ability to command and lead an infantry battalion was sorely lacking. I was pleased to learn later that
he became a competent and effective leader.

One day a young corporal came into the headquarters carrying a loaded pistol. He had either bartered something for it or had
picked it off some POW brought in for questioning. The corporal
was proud of his acquisition and was handling the pistol carelessly
when it accidently fired. The battalion commander had withdrawn
from the end of the CP tent where the operations and intelligence
sections worked and was seated on his cot at the opposite end of
the shelter. The round whizzed through the CP and passed to the
left of the CO's head and exited the tent, missing him only by inches.
I cannot remember the reaction of the staff except that we all yelled
at the corporal, but I clearly recall examining the small hole the
bullet had made in passage and knew that the commander realized how close he had been to death. The corporal was contrite

and apologized, and I believe the battalion S-2 shepherded him from the tent. Secretly, most of the staff was in general agreement that it would not have been a major disaster if the Old Man had been hit.

Within a week after going into the defensive position, tank-infantry patrols were sent forward of the MLR to determine the extent of enemy forces and where they were holed up. We seemed to be at a standstill, neither side willing to lash out in strength at the other. It even appeared that while each side had been able to get in some solid licks, at the same time both sides wanted to back off a bit. So with the exception of patrol action, very little was done. Some of us believed that we would fight north to the original line, the 38th Parallel, and then hold in place until negotiations to bring the war to an end commenced.

In any event, the UN command was not going to sit still forever in a defensive posture and wait for the Chinese to dictate the battle. Another offensive was soon to start, and on May 20 the division attacked in strength across the line in Operation Detonate. This was our final move north, although at the time no one would have believed it.

The orders were "to seek out and destroy the enemy," a directive that conjured up an aggressive reconnaissance in force to be undertaken by all units. That is precisely what happened. Spearheading forces slashed northward, fighting pitched battles, capturing large supply dumps, and inexorably forcing the Chinese and North Koreans farther away from the Han.

By June 1 all units had covered about forty miles and had crossed the 38th Parallel, and by June 12 they reached the vital Kumhwa area, the heart of the Communist so-called Iron Triangle. For all practical purposes, this was the beginning of the end of the fighting in Korea. While it continued into late summer, and some fierce battles were fought, for the most part it was confined to patrol and holding actions pending the outcome of the peace talks that commenced on July 10. While I had been involved in the planning activities for the battalion's effort, this action was to be my final assignment. I was going home.

14. Phase Omega

About the same time, having accumulated the requisite number of points that qualified me for rotation to the States, I was notified that my days were ending in Korea and that I was being sent home. This was very welcome news indeed, since I had not known the army had instituted such a plan. The program, which was to become popular with the men, allowed personnel to be transferred home on the basis of the time they had endured in Korea. As I recall, eligibility was based on points given for each month in the theater, with additional points given for wounds received. Because of my combined numbers, I was one of the early recipients. It was the second time I was grateful for having been wounded. Of course, one could opt out of the program and elect to stay put for some period by extending one's tour, and I suspect that some soldiers chose that option. I was not one of them.

I was excited about going home, to be with family and friends again, but I recognized the fact that leaving the battalion was not going to be easy. A large chunk of my young life had been spent there. I had been given a unique experience with comrades that would forever be a part of me wherever I went and whatever my future held. I had been robbed of at least a portion of my youth, never to be recaptured, a period of time spent in an unforgiving country that I would long remember. I knew that the sights and sounds, the failures and the few successes, the highs and the lows of combat would not easily be erased.

I was ambivalent about the rotation soon to come. On the one hand, I wanted to leave as quickly as possible, to escape from the daily threat of more engagements. On the other hand, as the number of days remaining slowly ticked down, I did not relish the idea of saying good-bye. I was a bit uncomfortable with the thought that I was leaving and others were being left behind.

We had fought together, known real hardship at times, and experienced the depression of numerous withdrawals and the exhilaration of going on the attack. Together, we had watched people die or be wounded, and my ambivalence was difficult to reconcile.

Members of the 24th Infantry Heavy Machine Gun Section clean weapons while in reserve June 5, 1951, after thirty-eight days in the line. *U.S. Army photograph*

I became quickly preoccupied with the idea of going home, and the thought of doing anything that might jeopardize my health or my life was primary. I "stacked arms"! This army expression describes the slackening of purpose of the soldier or the end of a drill. It is a command given to men to bring their rifles to a central location where they place the muzzles together in such a manner that one rifle supports another in a stack. The butt ends are on the ground, and this protects the weapon from getting dirty, which would happen if dropped into the mud or dust. I was instructed to turn in certain army gear. Perhaps there was a transition period between my notification and my departure date when I had to train my replacement, but I am not sure of that.

As time grew short, I packed my meager belongings and then made the rounds to say good-bye. As had happened when I returned to the battalion in February, I received congratulations on my good fortune and got a lot of good-natured static from many of the men. We exchanged addresses, made promises we would never keep, laughed together for the final time, probably shed a few hidden tears, and then I left by jeep for Inchon. I recall thinking this was the fourth time the division was attacking north again, and I prayed it would not suffer another traumatic retreat. There had been some pleasant times during my stay in Korea, but precious few. Everything is relative: a hot meal, a cold can of beer, a hot shower and change of clothing, and even a few humorous incidents spread over the year. They were worth remembering.

At Inchon, early that morning, I went aboard a navy troop ship that would take us to Japan. It was a clear, lovely morning, and we were ushered below to the mess hall for breakfast. The inviting smells wafted toward us – food for the asking. The steward assigned to us asked what we wanted for breakfast and suggested that almost anything was available. I ate a normal breakfast of steak and eggs, washed down with a pitcher of cold, fresh milk, but what I really craved above anything was ice cream. When I made my request, certain that no such thing existed aboard ship, I was served a gigantic bowl heaped to the top. I stuffed myself deliriously; it was a fabulous feast.

Shortly afterward we went on deck. It was the first day of June. I left Korea under a beautiful, blue sky, the same sky I had experienced when I arrived a year before. I cannot remember what my impression was as the ship slowly weighed anchor and we pushed away from the dock, except for one thing: I was ecstatic to be leaving and ready for whatever lay ahead. The Land of the Morning Calm slipped away as the ship picked up speed and sailed briskly down through the China Sea, around the horn, through the Korea Strait, and then on to Sasebo, Japan.

Good-bye, Korea; hello, Japan. While we waited for the troopship to take us home, we went through some kind of processing exercise. I believe we received physical examinations and were issued fresh uniforms, and I think we got a partial pay to take care of our personal needs. I had accrued nearly a year's pay, so I was well off financially. We were put up in barracks on the base but were allowed to go on our own to town and have a last party. There was a post exchange on the base, and most of us visited it for last-minute shopping.

At the time I was carrying two battle souvenirs – a Russian-made burp gun and a long rifle. I met a Major Lancaster, an air force-type, who generously offered to take the weapons with him when he flew back to the States. I was to retrieve them at the other end. Somehow, the transaction never occurred, and I was never able to pick up the pieces. There was a requirement for the barrels to be plugged, which I had taken care of before giving them away, so they are probably resting on some mantel as showpieces, since they can't be fired.

I clearly remember two things about the short stay in Sasebo. First, I could not overcome my fear of antipersonnel mines, and I was constantly looking at the ground as I walked, searching for the nonexistent mines that could no longer kill or maim me. It had been one of my greatest fears in Korea, and I could not stop this habit. Second, I found a hobby shop or store where I purchased balsa wood and glue and assorted tools so that I could design and build a model of a racing boat on the trip home. What was the subconscious and underlying reason for selecting a boat to build? I haven't the foggiest idea!

Epilogue

On July 10, 1952, a truce was proposed by North Korea, obviously with the approval of the Chinese. The first year of fighting had been brutal and deadly, perhaps beyond what had been anticipated by the governments of China and the Democratic People's Republic. North Korea had lost over half a million troops, and the Chinese suffered nearly a million killed. Now both sides came to the negotiation table, and peace talks commenced.

For the next two years the talks focused on designation of the final line to be drawn between North and South Korea and on POW exchange. Fighting continued, however, as more battles were fought, primarily for the purpose of gaining advantageous ground positions. Finally, the Korean War ended in a stalemate, and an uneasy peace descended on the peninsula.

The Korean War, one of the bloodiest in history, had a major impact on many people. It affected 157,000 American lives directly in three years of fighting – those who were killed, wounded, or lost in action. Of this number, the majority were killed or wounded in the first year. The dead alone number nearly 55,000, a figure not much lower than those killed in Vietnam during ten years of that war. Another 8,000 Americans still are unaccounted and are presumed to be lost forever. It has been reported that no American succeeded in escaping from the POW camps, and many prisoners died from cruelty, malnutrition, or exposure to the climate; many died on the long, brutal marches north. Yet ours was the forgotten war.

It took place that first year against a backdrop of U.S. political indecision, a downgraded U.S. military capability, and a numerically strong enemy who knew how to fight. For us, the heartache and frustration of attacking and withdrawing (frequently over the same bloody ground) lent credence to the thought that Korea was a gigantic checkerboard on which we were moved in every direction in order to reach a draw.

On both sides of the 38th Parallel there was great destruction and loss of life. The tiny country of South Korea survived thirty-seven months of war. The price was a devastated countryside, a ruined economy, and more than a million dead. Several million more were made homeless, and damage throughout the country exceeded a billion dollars.

In the aftermath of the fighting, South Korea, which possessed a large and mainly unskilled labor force, rose from the ashes to become a fast-developing, labor-rich, newly industrialized country. It has worked relentlessly to convert a labor force from an agrarian orientation to that of an industrial focus. Korea's isolation has ended, at least in the South. The Hermit Kingdom, which opened its doors to foreign trade in the late 1800s, now has an industrial base from which it produces and ships electronics, ships, textiles, and chemicals around the world. One-third of its population of 43 million are employed, 75 percent of whom are working in the manufactured goods and services sectors. The Republic of Korea continues to have one of the world's highest growth rates in gross national product. It is a country in which the tail of industrial progress is wagging the economic tiger.

Yet all is not serene and peaceful in the Land of the Morning Calm. Two modern armies, each with more than half a million troops, face one another, ready and willing to fight a war. Political dissent is frequent and vociferous. Labor strikes, student discontent, and peasant revolts have quickly been met with authoritarian power exercised by the government. Labor organizers, clergy, opposition-party politicians, and the omnipresent student demonstrators appear willing to take on any perceived injustice in order to bring pressure on the government to correct the wrong.

The Cold War continues on both sides of the Demilitarized Zone, even though a unified Korea would offer advantages to each half. The natural resources of the North would give greater impetus to continued industrialization in the South, and both would benefit from the whole. How ironic it is, then, that the separation of political entities has effectively robbed the economic potential of the entire peninsula. Still, as was the case in 1950, the two Koreas exist side by side, each with a different economic-political system controlling its fate.

Today, there is no peace treaty to end the war, no talk of one, no reunification of the country. The Korean War was not an accident of history as some have alleged. The line, near where it all started, remains a no-man's-land, fortified and manned, where men may still be killed as they wait for peace. The demilitarized zone winds across the neck of Korea from the Han River estuary in the west to the East Sea, slightly below the 39th Parallel. Through the center of the four-kilometer strip runs the Military Demarcation Line, across which the opposing forces may not move.

In the Joint Security Area in Panmunjom, a farm village where the armistice was signed in 1953, the UN countries, headed by the U.S. representative, continue a dialogue to end the war peacefully. The failure of the parties to reach agreement is a sad commentary on their inability to honor the men and women of sixteen nations who gave their lives in Korea.

Forty years later, the pattern of terrorist attacks, border incidents, propaganda releases, and even underground tunnels to move men and equipment are reminiscent of the events of 1950. Today, the United States maintains a force of less than forty-five thousand troops stationed in the South, but negotiations between the Republic of Korea and the United States may cause a reduction in force levels, with the concomitant effect of lowering the military presence and stability in the region. And if we leave, what then? It seems easy to forget about all of Korea. We have scant information and less insight into Communist North Korea.

As for South Korea, the vast majority of Americans know as little about it as they did in 1950. Many picture the Republic of Korea as a critical mass in the world economy, ready to explode and spread its products, in the pattern of the Japanese, all over the globe. A small group of economists, international business leaders, top managers of multinational corporations, and a few military planners know South Korea more intimately and where it stands today in world affairs. This group sees a Pacific-rim tiger with sharp teeth, and a tenaciousness of purpose ready to take on the newcomers invading its turf.

As the winds of change flow across the Western Europe and the former Soviet Union, and thence down through Manchuria and into Korea, what happens next? Will the sounds of reunification of the German states echo loud enough so that the two Koreas will hear and follow the call to reunite themselves? Will the leadership of South Korea heed the warnings of their own people and follow the call to democracy, thereby setting the stage for one united nation?

Only recently has the leadership of what was the Soviet Union made overtures to talk with South Korea, and several peace feelers have been extended by North Korea to the United States. More directly, the North Korean rulers have initiated discussion with South

Korea to determine if the parties can reconcile their differences. Will these efforts result in a final solution?

Four and one-half decades ago we, the United States, drew the line separating the two halves. In expediency or naïveté, we divided the Korean nation as the Japanese surrendered. Now we have the opportunity to seek some dynamic solution to the problem. We must encourage, cajole, or influence the South Korea Republic to get on with the task of becoming a free democracy. Likewise, we must do all we can to move North Korea to adopt attitudes consistent with glasnost and perestroika. We must conduct creative diplomacy in every sense of the word. We owe this to all Korean peoples, North and South.

If we cannot move them together in spirit and in law, then we must be prepared to fight once more, perhaps before the twenty-first century comes into view. For the same scenario, on the same peninsular slope, could easily be played again, and the flowering success story of South Korea today may be flung into the dustbin of history tomorrow.

24th Infantry Regiment

The history of the 24th Infantry Regiment dates from July 28, 1866, when it was established as a separate regiment by an act of Congress. The unit was activated with Negro personnel.

On November 1, 1869, a consolidation of the 38th and 41st occurred, and the new, single unit was designated the 24th Infantry Regiment.

In 1880 the 24th was sent into Indian Territory, where it participated in the campaign against the Comanche Indians.

In the Spanish-American War battle for San Juan Hill, which it captured, the 24th distinguished itself as a unit of the 3d Brigade, 1st Infantry Division.

During the Philippines insurrection, the 24th served in the islands from July, 1899, to August, 1902.

In the spring of 1916 the unit was ordered to Mexico with the "Punitive Expedition." In 1922 the regiment was reassigned to Fort Benning, Georgia. In March, 1940, a reorganization of the military authorized the 24th to be reactivated to participate in World War II, where it served in the Pacific Theater of Operations. The regiment received the surrender of the Japanese garrison on the island of Aka-Shima in 1945.

Soon after, the regiment joined the 25th Infantry Division and served in the army of occupation of Japan.

In early July, 1950, the unit was ordered to Korea and went into action immediately. It is credited with the first victory of the war, at Yechon.

The regiment was deactivated on October 1, 1951, one month short of its eighty-second birthday.

Composition of Second Platoon

Sergeant Nollie – platoon sgt.

1st Squad
Sgt. Mims, leader
Wakefield
Howard
Griffin
Pirtle
Williams
Smith
Rolling
plus 3 ROKs

2d Squad
Sgt. Hicks, leader
Wilson
Asbury
Shannon
Gill
Durnell
Wetherford
Wiliford
Williams, F.
Spear

3d Squad
Sgt. McRoberts, leader
Archard
Doss
Grandy
Lewis
Mose
Rhodes
Roberson (Robie)
Wheat
plus 3 ROKs

4th Squad
Sgt. Rochelle, leader
Clark
Dedeaux
Giles
Haskins
Smith, A.
Stearns
Wright
Ballard
plus 2 ROKs

Republic of Korea soldiers (ROKs)
Kim Pyong Sum, interpreter
Byun Tae Yub
Sin Chung Rak
Lee Wun Bae
Kim Man Kab

Kim Tu Sik
Kim Hong Ju
Dee Pong Sun
Sun Mung Sik
Che Cha Bong

The composition of the platoon changed many times, as casualties ran high. The squad leaders remained with me for the entire time, with the exception of Sergeant Mims, who was killed later in the fighting.

Index